DEMOCRACIES

DEMOCRACIES

Patterns of Majoritarian and Consensus Government in Twenty-One Countries

AREND LIJPHART

YALE UNIVERSITY PRESS
NEW HAVEN and LONDON

Published with assistance from the
Louis Stern Memorial Fund.

Designed by James J. Johnson
and set in Melior Roman type by
Graphic Composition Inc.
Printed in the United States of America by
Courier Westford, Inc., Westford, Mass.

Library of Congress Cataloging in Publication Data

Lijphart, Arend.
  Democracies: patterns of majoritarian and
  consensus government in twenty-one countries.

  Includes bibliographical references and index.
  1. Democracy.   2. Comparative government.
  I. Title.
  JC421.L537 1984   321.8   83–14639
  ISBN 0–300–03182–3

20   19   18   17   16

FOR GISELA

Qui potest esse vita vitalis,
quae non in amicae
mutua benevolentia conquiescit?

Contents

Figures and Tables

ix

Preface

This book is a systematic comparison of the two basic models of democracy: majoritarian (or Westminster) and consensus. I have borrowed this pair of contrasting terms from Robert G. Dixon, Jr., and my definitions are similar, though not identical, to his. The components of consensus democracy, according to Dixon, include "federalism, separation of powers, the bicameral structure of legislatures, with each house representing a somewhat different electorate and requiring a double scrutiny of all measures, the committee and seniority system used within legislatures, the state-based rather than nation-based political party system, requirements for extraordinary majorities to enact certain kinds of measures, the executive veto power and the power to override it with an extraordinary majority, and numerous other formal arrangements and informal practices."[1] This list of characteristics overlaps my eight elements of consensus democracy to an important extent.

My concept of consensus democracy is also inspired by and

1. Robert G. Dixon, Jr., *Democratic Representation: Reapportionment in Law and Politics* (New York: Oxford University Press, 1968), p. 10. See also the comparison between Madisonian and populistic democracy in Robert A. Dahl, *A Preface to Democratic Theory* (Chicago: University of Chicago Press, 1956).

related to my earlier work on consociational democracy.[2] In this book, I use the term *consensus* rather than *consociational* not just because the former is shorter—and easier to pronounce!— than the latter, but because there are crucial differences between their meanings. For one thing, my earlier writings took consociational democracy as their point of departure and contrasted it with majority rule; here I start out with an analysis of the majoritarian model, from which I derive the consensus model as its logical opposite. Furthermore, the four characteristics of consociational democracy—grand coalition, segmental autonomy, proportionality, and minority veto—are clearly recognizable in, but not coincident with, the eight characteristics of consensus democracy described in this book.

■ ■ ■

I presented a preliminary version of the first two chapters of the book as a paper to the International Workshop on "Political Science in the 1980s" organized by the Instituto de Estudos Econômicos, Sociais e Políticos de São Paulo, Brazil, in November 1981. I am grateful to the participants for their helpful comments. Among the other many helpful critics, too many to list exhaustively, I should like to single out Nathaniel L. Beck, Robert G. Cushing, and Adam Przeworski for special thanks. I am also grateful to Kenneth R. Mayer for his research assistance and to Monica Ann Paskvan, Barbara J. Sutera, and Barbara K. Ziering for typing the manuscript.

Some of the chapters of the book draw on my earlier work. I acknowledge with gratitude the permission to reprint a few passages from my articles "Power-Sharing versus Majority Rule: Patterns of Cabinet Formation in Twenty Democracies," *Government and Opposition* 16, no. 4 (Autumn 1981):395–413 (chapter 4), and "Consociation and Federation: Conceptual and Empirical Links," *Canadian Journal of Political Science* 12, no. 3 (Septem-

2. See, in particular, Arend Lijphart, *Democracy in Plural Societies: A Comparative Exploration* (New Haven: Yale University Press, 1977).

ber 1979):499–515 (chapter 10); and from my chapters "Political Parties: Ideologies and Programs," in David Butler, Howard R. Penniman, and Austin Ranney, eds., *Democracy at the Polls: A Comparative Study of Competitive National Elections* (Washington, D.C.: American Enterprise Institute, 1981), 26–51 (chapter 8), "Introduction: The Belgian Example of Cultural Coexistence in Comparative Perspective," in Arend Lijphart, ed., *Conflict and Coexistence in Belgium: The Dynamics of a Culturally Divided Society* (Berkeley: Institute of International Studies, University of California, 1981), 1–12 (chapter 2), and "Os Modelos Majoritário e Consociacional da Democracia: Contrastes e Illustrações," in Bolivar Lamounier, ed., *A Ciência Política nos Anos 80* (Brazil: Editora da Universidade de Brasília, 1982), 95–115 (chapters 1 and 2).

The Westminster Model of Democracy 1

DEMOCRATIC IDEALS AND REALITIES

The literal meaning of democracy—government by the people—is probably also the most basic and most widely used definition. The one major amendment that is necessary when we speak of democracy at the national level in modern large-scale nation-states is that the acts of government are usually performed not directly by the citizens but indirectly by representatives whom they elect on a free and equal basis. Although elements of direct democracy can be found even in some large democratic states (as we shall see in chapter 12), democracy is usually representative democracy: government by the freely elected representatives of the people.

Democracy may be defined not only as government *by* the people but also, in President Abraham Lincoln's famous formulation, as goverment *for* the people—that is, government in accordance with the people's preferences. An ideal democratic government would be one whose actions were *always* in *perfect* correspondence with the preferences of *all* its citizens. Such complete responsiveness in government has never existed and may never be achieved, but it can serve as an ideal to which democratic regimes should aspire. It can also be regarded as the end of a scale on which the degree of democratic responsiveness of different regimes may be measured. The subject of this book is not the ideal of democracy but the operation of actual democracies that approximate the ideal relatively closely—and that Robert Dahl calls "polyarchies" in order to distinguish them from ideal democracy.[1] These democratic regimes are characterized not by perfect responsiveness but by a high degree of it: their actions have been in *relatively close* correspondence with the wishes of *relatively many* of their citizens for a *long period of time*. Both definitions of democracy will also be used later to distinguish the two basic *types* of democracy.

As Dahl has shown, a reasonably responsive democracy can exist only if at least eight institutional guarantees are present:

1. Freedom to form and join organizations;
2. Freedom of expression;
3. The right to vote;
4. Eligibility for public office;
5. The right of political leaders to compete for support and votes;
6. Alternative sources of information;
7. Free and fair elections;
8. Institutions for making government policies depend on votes and other expressions of preference.[2]

The first six of these embody the classic democratic right of liberty, especially the freedoms of speech and assembly, and they also imply the second classic democratic value of equality. In the democracies treated in this book, these rights are securely guaranteed without major variations between different countries. Guarantees 7 and 8 are also provided, but substantial differences occur in the way elections and other institutions and practices are organized to insure responsive government. This book will

1. Robert A. Dahl, *Polyarchy: Participation and Opposition* (New Haven: Yale University Press, 1971). See also John D. May, "Defining Democracy: A Bid for Coherence and Consensus," *Political Studies* 26, no. 1, (March 1978):1–14.
2. Dahl, *Polyarchy*, p. 3.

focus on the variety of formal and informal institutions and practices that are used to translate citizen preferences into public
policies. While recognizing and describing these differences, I
will also try to discover patterns and regularities, and I will argue
that both the variations and the regularities can be interpreted in
terms of two diametrically opposite models of democracy: the
majoritarian model (or the Westminster model) and the consensus model.

The majoritarian and consensus models of democracy differ
on eight dimensions. These will be discussed in a preliminary
fashion in the remainder of this chapter and in chapter 2, and
they will be analyzed in greater depth in the nine chapters that
comprise the bulk of the book (chapters 4 to 12). The twenty-two
empirical cases of democratic regimes that will be compared—
mainly the democracies of the North Atlantic area but also including Israel, Japan, Australia, and New Zealand—will be
introduced in chapter 3. There are twenty-one countries but
twenty-two democratic regimes because the French Fourth and
Fifth Republics will be treated as separate cases. The concluding
chapter (chapter 13) will summarize the overall patterns of democracy that we find in our set of democracies and consider the
question: to what extent are the two contrasting models of democracy not only logically coherent but also empirical models?

The principal emphasis throughout the book will be on the
interrelationships among the different majoritarian and consensual characteristics. In the concluding chapter, I shall also try to
explain the differential incidence of majoritarian and consensual
patterns in the twenty-two democratic regimes in terms of the
countries' cultural and structural characteristics: the degree to
which they are plural (divided) societies, the sizes of their populations, and Anglo-American versus other cultural influences.
An additional question worth asking is: how does the type of
democratic regime, majoritarian or consensual, affect its performance? My analysis will suggest that majoritarian democracy
is especially appropriate for, and works best in, homogeneous

societies, whereas consensus democracy is more suitable for plural societies. Otherwise, there is relatively little variation in how well the democracies analyzed in this book perform. As chapter 3 will show, my cases of democracy were chosen according to exacting standards: they are all democracies of long standing and must also be judged as basically successful. Indeed, one of the principal messages of this book is that there are many different ways of successfully running a democracy.[3]

THE WESTMINSTER MODEL: NINE MAJORITARIAN ELEMENTS

The essence of the Westminster model is majority rule. The model can be seen as the most obvious solution to the dilemma of what is meant by "the people" in our definition of democracy. Who will do the governing and to whose interests should the government be responsive when the people are in disagreement and have divergent preferences? One answer is: the majority of the people. Its great merit is that any other answer, such as the requirement of unanimity or a qualified majority, entails minority rule—or at least a minority veto—and that government by the majority and in accordance with the majority's wishes comes closer to the democratic ideal than government by and responsive to a minority. The alternative answer to the dilemma is: as many people as possible. This is the essence of the consensus model; as we shall see in more detail in the next chapter, its rules

3. Democratic performance has also been stubbornly resistant to meaningful and precise measurement. In the strongest attempt so far to measure how well democracies perform, G. Bingham Powell uses three indicators: executive stability or durability, voting turnout, and the absence of large-scale violence. Chapters 5 and 7 will show, however, that executive durability is not a good measure of democratic performance at all; it merely indicates the strength of the executive in relation to the legislature. Voting turnout is a weak and peripheral aspect of performance. And large-scale violence is fortunately a very rare occurrence in all of our democracies. See G. Bingham Powell, Jr., *Contemporary Democracies: Participation, Stability, and Violence* (Cambridge, Mass.: Harvard University Press, 1982).

and institutions aim at broad participation in government and broad agreement on the policies that the government should pursue.

In this book the term *Westminster model* will be used interchangeably with *majoritarian model* to refer to a general model of democracy. It may also be used more narrowly to denote the main characteristics of *British* parliamentary and governmental institutions; Great Britain's Parliament meets in the Palace of Westminster in London. The British version of the Westminster model is both the original and the best-known example of this model. Is is also widely admired. Richard Rose points out that, "with confidence born of continental isolation, Americans have come to assume that their institutions—the Presidency, Congress and the Supreme Court—are the prototype of what should be adopted elsewhere."[4] But American political scientists, especially those in the field of comparative politics, have tended to hold the British system of government in at least equally high esteem.[5]

One famous political scientist who fervently admired the Westminster model was President Woodrow Wilson. In his early writings he went so far as to urge the abolition of presidential government and the adoption of British-style parliamentary government in the United States. Such views have also been held by many other non-British observers of British politics, and many features of the Westminster model have been exported to other countries: Canada, Australia, New Zealand, and most of Britain's colonies in Asia and Africa at the moment of their independence. Wilson referred to parliamentary government in accordance with the Westminster model as "the world's fashion."[6]

The Westminster model consists of the following nine inter-

4. Richard Rose, "A Model Democracy?", in Richard Rose, ed., *Lessons from America: An Exploration* (New York: Wiley, 1974), p. 131.

5. Dennis Kavanagh, "An American Science of British Politics," *Political Studies* 22, no. 3 (September 1974):251–70.

6. Woodrow Wilson, "Committee or Cabinet Government," *Overland Monthly*, January 1884, quoted by Walter Lippmann in his introduction to Wood-

related elements, which will be illustrated by features of the British political system—deliberately described in rather stark terms, the necessary nuances to be added later—particularly as it operated in the period from 1945 to 1970:

1. Concentration of executive power: one-party and bare-majority cabinets. The most powerful organ of British government is the cabinet. It is usually composed of members of the party that has the majority of seats in the House of Commons, and the minority is not included. Coalition cabinets are rare. Because in the British two-party system the two principal parties are of approximately equal strength, the party that wins the elections usually represents no more than a narrow majority, and the minority is relatively large. Hence the British one-party and bare-majority cabinet is the perfect embodiment of the principle of majority rule: it wields vast amounts of political power to rule as the representative of and in the interest of a majority that is not of overwhelming proportions. A large minority is excluded from power and condemned to the role of opposition.

2. Fusion of power and cabinet dominance. In his enduring classic, *The English Constitution,* first published in 1867, Walter Bagehot states that "the close union, the nearly complete fusion of the executive and legislative powers" is the key explanation of the efficient operation of the British government.[7] Britain has a parliamentary system of government, which means that the cabinet is dependent on the confidence of Parliament—in contrast with a presidential system of government, exemplified by the United States, in which the presidential executive cannot normally be removed by the legislature (except by impeach-

---

row Wilson, *Congressional Government: A Study in American Politics* (New York: Meridian Books, 1956), p. 13.

7. Walter Bagehot, *The English Constitution* (London: World's Classics, 1955), p. 9.

ment). In theory, because the House of Commons can vote a cabinet out of office, it "controls" the cabinet. In reality, however, the relationship is reversed. Because the cabinet is composed of the leaders of a cohesive majority party in the House of Commons, it is normally backed by the majority in the House of Commons, and it can confidently count on staying in office and getting its legislative proposals approved. The cabinet is clearly dominant vis-à-vis Parliament.

3. Asymmetric bicameralism. The British parliament consists of two chambers: the House of Commons, which is popularly elected, and the House of Lords, which consists mainly of members of the hereditary nobility. Their relationship is an asymmetric one: almost all legislative power belongs to the House of Commons. The only power that the House of Lords retains is the power to delay legislation: money bills can be delayed for one month and all other bills for one year. It may be argued that a purer version of the Westminster model would be characterized by unicameralism, because a single chamber dominated by a majority party and by a one-party cabinet would be a more perfect manifestation of majority rule. Britain comes very close to this ideal: in everyday discussion, "Parliament" refers almost exclusively to the House of Commons. British asymmetric bicameralism may also be called near unicameralism.

4. Two-party system. British politics is dominated by two large parties: the Conservative party and the Labour party. There are other parties, in particular the Liberals, that contest elections and win seats in the House of Commons, but they are not large enough to be the overall victors. The bulk of the seats are captured by the two major parties, and they form the cabinets: the Labour party from 1945 to 1951, 1964 to 1970, and 1974 to 1979, and the Conservatives from 1951 to 1964, 1970 to 1974, and from 1979 on.

5. One-dimensional party system. The principal politically significant difference that divides the British and their main parties is disagreement about socioeconomic policies: on the left–right spectrum, Labour represents the left-of-center and the Conservative party the right-of-center preferences. This difference is also reflected in the pattern of voters' support for the parties in elections to the House of Commons: working-class voters tend to cast their ballots for Labour candidates and middle-class voters tend to support Conservative candidates. There are other differences, of course, but these do not have a major effect on the composition of the House of Commons and the cabinet. For instance, religious differences between Protestants and Catholics are no longer politically salient. Regional and ethnic differences, particularly Scottish national sentiments, are of greater importance, but they do not present a grave threat to the hegemony of the Conservative and Labour parties. British society is highly homogeneous, and the socioeconomic issue dimension is the only dimension on which the main parties clearly and consistently diverge.

6. Plurality system of elections. The 650 members of the House of Commons are elected in single-member districts according to the plurality method, which in Britain is often referred to as the "first past the post" system: the candidate with the majority vote or, if there is no majority, with the largest minority vote wins.

7. Unitary and centralized government. Local governments in Britain perform a series of important functions, but they are the creatures of the central government and their powers are not constitutionally guaranteed (as in a federal system). Moreover, they are financially dependent on the central government. This unitary and centralized system means that there are no clearly designated geographical and functional areas from which the parliamentary majority and the cabinet are barred.

8. Unwritten constitution and parliamentary sovereignty. Britain has a constitution that is "unwritten" in the sense that there is not a single written document that specifies the composition and powers of the governmental institutions and the rights of citizens. These are defined instead in a number of basic laws, customs, and conventions. Parliament will normally obey these constitutional rules, but it is not formally bound by them. Even the basic laws have no special status, and they can be changed by Parliament in the same way as any other laws. The courts do not have the power of judicial review. Parliament is the ultimate, or sovereign, authority. Parliamentary sovereignty is a vital ingredient of the majoritarianism of the Westminster model, because it means that there are no formal restrictions on the power of the majority of the House of Commons.

9. Exclusively representative democracy. Parliamentary sovereignty also means that, because all power is concentrated in the House of Commons acting as the people's representative, there is no room for any element of direct democracy such as the referendum. In the words of one constitutional expert, "referenda are foreign to British constitutional practice."[8] Parliamentary sovereignty and popular sovereignty are incompatible, and British democracy is therefore an exclusively representative democracy.

BRITISH DEVIATIONS FROM
THE WESTMINSTER MODEL

The nine characteristics of the Westminster model together make the model thoroughly majoritarian. But the power of the majority should not be exaggerated. In Britain, majority rule does not entail majority tyranny. Although there are no formal limitations

8. D. C. M. Yardley, "The Effectiveness of the Westminster Model of Constitution," in George W. Keeton and Georg Schwarzenberger, eds., *Year Book of World Affairs 1977* (London: Stevens and Sons, 1977), p. 348.

on parliamentary power—and hence no formal limits to what
the majority of the House of Commons can do—strong informal
customs do restrain the majority. The rights and freedoms of the
people are not violated, and minorities are not suppressed. In
the House of Commons, the minority is treated with respect, and
it is also customary that the leader of the opposition be consulted
by the cabinet on questions that are especially important or sensitive. British democracy, although majoritarian, is tolerant and
civil.

It should also be emphasized that British politics was in close
conformity with the Westminster model only in the twenty-five
years from 1945 to 1970. From 1918, when the admission of
women to the suffrage (although still not on the same basis as
men) marked the beginning of a fully democratic system, until
1945 and again in the period since 1970, there have been significant deviations from the Westminster model of majoritarian democracy with regard to almost all of the model's nine characteristics.

*1. Concentration of executive power: one-party and bare-
majority cabinets.* As David Butler writes, "single-party government is the British norm. Politicians and writers on politics
assume that, in all but exceptional circumstances, one party will
have a Parliamentary majority and will conduct the nation's affairs." But, he continues, "clear-cut single-party government has
been much less prevalent than many would suppose."[9] In fact,
one-party majority cabinets have held office for only about 60
percent of the years between 1918 and 1980. Most of the deviations from the norm—coalitions of two or more parties and minority cabinets—occurred from 1918 to 1945. The most recent
instance of a clear and explicit coalition cabinet was the 1940–
45 wartime coalition formed by the Conservatives, who had a
parliamentary majority, with the Labour and Liberal parties, un-

9. David Butler, "Conclusion," in David Butler, ed., *Coalitions in British
Politics* (New York: St. Martin's Press, 1978), p. 112.

der Conservative Prime Minister Winston Churchill. There were two minority Labour cabinets in the 1970s. In the parliamentary election of March 1974, the Labour party won a plurality but not a majority of the seats and formed a minority government dependent on all other parties not uniting to defeat it. New elections were held in October of the same year in which Labour won an outright, albeit narrow, majority of the seats; but this majority was eroded by defections and by-election defeats, and the Labour cabinet again became a minority cabinet in 1976. The 1970s also provide an example of a two-party coalition. In 1977, the minority Labour cabinet negotiated a formal pact with the thirteen Liberals in the House of Commons in order to regain a parliamentary majority: the Liberals agreed to support the cabinet in exchange for consultation on legislative proposals prior to their submission to Parliament, but no Liberals entered the cabinet. This so-called Lab-Lib pact lasted until 1978.

 2. *Fusion of power and cabinet dominance.* Strong cabinet leadership depends on majority support in the House of Commons and on the cohesiveness of the majority party. When either or both of these conditions are absent, cabinets lose much of their predominant position. Since 1970 there has been a significant increase in the frequency of parliamentary defeats of important proposals introduced by both majority and minority cabinets. This has even caused a change in the traditional view that cabinets must resign or dissolve the House of Commons and call for new elections if they suffer a defeat on either a parliamentary vote of no confidence or a major bill of central importance to the cabinet. After the frequent cabinet defeats of the 1970s, the new unwritten rule is that only an explicit vote of no confidence necessitates resignation or new elections.[10] After suffering but sur-

    10. Leon D. Epstein, "What Happened to the British Party Model?", *American Political Science Review* 74, no. 1 (March 1980):pp. 9–22; Philip Norton, "The Changing Face of the British House of Commons in the 1970s," *Legislative Studies Quarterly* 5, no. 3 (August 1980):333–57.

viving many legislative defeats, Prime Minister James Callaghan's minority Labour cabinet was finally brought down by such a no confidence vote in 1979.

3. Asymmetric bicameralism. The one-year limit on the power of the House of Lords to delay the passage of ordinary non-money bills was established in 1949. Between the major reform of 1911 and 1949 the Lords' delaying power was about two years, but in the entire period since 1911 they have usually refrained from imposing long delays. No changes have taken place in recent years, although the overwhelmingly Conservative House of Lords became somewhat more assertive during the periods of weak Labour cabinets in the 1970s. This has also increased the sentiments in the Labour party to abolish the House of Lords altogether—and thus to change near-unicameralism into pure and complete unicameralism.

4. Two-party system. The interwar years were a transitional period during which the Labour party replaced the Liberals as one of the two big parties. In the 1945 election, the Labour and Conservative parties together won about 85 percent of the votes and 92.5 percent of the seats in the House of Commons. The hegemony of these two parties was even clearer in the seven elections from 1950 to 1970: jointly they never won less than 87.5 percent of the votes and 98 percent of the seats. But their support declined considerably in the 1970s: although they managed to win roughly 95 percent of the parliamentary seats in the three elections held after 1970, their joint share of the popular vote was only about 75 percent in the two elections in 1974 and about 81 percent in the 1979 election. The Liberals were the main beneficiaries. Although they succeeded in winning only a disappointing number of seats (14, 13, and 11 respectively in the three elections), they captured about 19 percent of the votes in the two elections of 1974 and about 14 percent in 1979. In the early 1980s, a graver threat to the two-party system appeared in the form of the Social Democratic party, mainly consisting of defectors from Labour. Only about half a year after the new party's launching in 1981, the London *Economist* wrote: "Its alliance with the Liberals will give the two parties at least a sporting chance of being Britain's biggest political entity in Westminster after the next general election."[11]

5. One-dimensional party system. From about 1970 on, it has become increasingly clear that it is a mistake to regard British society as basically homogeneous. Especially Scotland, Wales, and Northern Ireland—the non-English regions of what is officially called the United Kingdom of Great Britain and Northern Ireland—contribute considerable diversity in political attitudes and preferences. In 1964, Rose was the spokesman of the majority of scholarly observers of British politics when he wrote: "Today politics in the United Kingdom is greatly simplified by the absence of major cleavages along the lines of ethnic groups, language, or religion." But six years later he described the United Kingdom more accurately as "a multi-national state."[12] For the party system this means that social class is not the only, although still the most important, dimension of differentiation. The ethnic factor has become especially strong in Scotland: in the October 1974 elections, the Scottish National party received more than 30 percent of the votes cast in Scotland and 11 House of Commons seats, almost as many as the Liberals. Its fortunes have somewhat declined since then, but in 1979 it still won two parliamentary seats, the same number that was won by the Welsh nationalists. Religion has not entirely disappeared as a determinant of voting behavior either: in fact, the Protestant–Catholic difference in Northern Ireland is the overwhelmingly dominant

11. *The Economist*, December 5, 1981, p. 69.
12. Richard Rose, *Politics in England: An Interpretation* (Boston: Little Brown, 1964), p. 10; Richard Rose, *The United Kingdom as a Multi-National State*, Occasional Paper Number 6 (Glasgow: Survey Research Centre, University of Strathclyde, 1970).

division separating the parties and their supporters in that part of the United Kingdom.

6. *Plurality system of elections.* No changes have been made in the plurality single-member district method of electing the House of Commons, but this electoral system has come under increasing criticism, mainly because of the disproportional results it produced in the 1970s.[13] For instance, the Labour party won an absolute parliamentary majority of 319 out of 635 seats with only 39.3 percent of the total vote in the October 1974 elections, while the Liberals won only 13 seats with 18.6 percent of the vote—almost half of the Labour vote. The Liberals are understandably eager to introduce some form of proportional representation, but the Conservative and Labour parties remain committed to the plurality method. It should be pointed out, however, that proportional representation was adopted for Northern Ireland elections after the outbreak of Protestant–Catholic strife by a Conservative cabinet in the early 1970s, and that the subsequent Labour cabinets continued this policy. The *principle* of proportionality is no longer anathema.

7. *Unitary and centralized government.* The United Kingdom remains a unitary state, but can it also be described as a highly centralized state? Two exceptions should be noted. One is that Northern Ireland was ruled by its own parliament and cabinet with a very high degree of autonomy—more than what most states in federal systems have—from 1921, when the Republic of Ireland became independent, until the imposition of direct rule from London in 1972. The second exception is the gradual movement toward greater autonomy for Scotland and Wales—"devolution," in British parlance.

13. S. E. Finer, "Introduction: Adversary Politics and Electoral Reform," in S. E. Finer, ed., *Adversary Politics and Electoral Reform* (London: Anthony Wigram, 1975) pp. 6–12.

8. Unwritten constitution and parliamentary sovereignty. Britain's entry into the European Economic Community (Common Market), which is a supranational instead of merely an international organization, in 1973 entailed the acceptance of the European Community's laws and institutions as higher authorities than the national parliament with regard to several areas of policy. Because sovereignty means supreme and ultimate authority, the British Parliament can therefore no longer be regarded as fully sovereign. Britain's membership in the European Community has also introduced a potential right of judicial review both for the Community's Court of Justice and for British courts: "Parliament's supremacy is challenged by the right of the Community institutions to legislate for the United Kingdom (without the prior consent of Parliament) and by the right of the courts to rule on the admissibility (in terms of Community law) of future acts of Parliament."[14]

9. Exclusively representative democracy. The rule that the referendum is incompatible with the Westminster model was also broken in the 1970s, when Parliament voted to let the people decide the controversial issue of Britain's membership in the European Community. In a unique referendum in 1975—the only national referendum ever held in the United Kingdom—the British electorate voted to keep Britain in the Community.

In one final respect, the simple picture of an omnipotent one-party cabinet using its parliamentary majority to carry out the mandate it has received from the voters is, and has always been, false and misleading. It implies that the cabinet can formulate and execute its policies without the aid of other forces in society and without encountering any significant resistance from these forces. In fact, it has long been recognized that in Britain

14. David Coombs, "British Government and the European Community," in Dennis Kavanagh and Richard Rose, eds., *New Trends in British Politics: Issues for Research* (London: Sage, 1977), p. 88.

and other democracies many organized groups compete for influence, and that they tend to check and balance not only each other but also the political parties and the government. This pluralist view of the political process has been strengthened in recent years by the "corporate pluralists," who have called attention to the fact that especially the major economic interest groups have become closely and continually involved in decision-making, and that governments have become extremely dependent on these new partners. Although the Conservative cabinet still had a comfortable parliamentary majority in early 1974, the striking mineworkers successfully defied it and forced it to call an election—which it lost. The misleading image of cabinet omnipotence has been replaced by the new image—probably also somewhat exaggerated—of "the *illusion* of governmental authority."[15]

THE WESTMINSTER MODEL IN NEW ZEALAND

The Westminster model, originated and developed in the British political setting, has also been highly influential outside of the United Kingdom. In particular, many of the model's features have been exported to the members of the British Commonwealth, such as Canada, Australia, and New Zealand. Canada and Australia deviate from the model in several basic respects—for one thing, they are both federal systems—but New Zealand is a virtually perfect example of the Westminster model of democracy.

1. Concentration of executive power: one-party and bare-majority cabinets. New Zealand had a wartime coalition cabinet from 1915 to 1919, and another coalition was in power from 1931 to 1935. From 1935 on, however, New Zealand politics has been dominated by two large parties—the Labour party and the National party—which have alternated in office. All cabinets since 1935 have been one-party cabinets. Moreover, all of these cabi-

15. Norman H. Keehn, "Great Britain: The Illusion of Governmental Authority," *World Politics* 30, no. 4 (July 1978):538–62 (italics added).

nets have been supported by clear but not overwhelming majorities in Parliament: the number of seats won by the majority party
has usually been between 50 and 60 percent and, from 1938 on,
never more than two-thirds of the total number of parliamentary
seats.

2. *Fusion of power and cabinet dominance.* In this respect, too, New Zealand is a perfect example of the Westminster
model. It has a parliamentary system with a cabinet dependent
on the confidence of Parliament, but, as a recent survey of New
Zealand politics states, the "rigidly disciplined two-party system
has contributed to the concentration of power within the Cabinet, formed from amongst the Members of Parliament . . . belonging to the majority party."[16]

3. *Unicameralism.* For about a century, New Zealand had a
bicameral legislature, consisting of an elected lower house and
an appointed upper house, but the latter gradually lost power. Its
abolition is 1950 changed the asymmetrical bicameral system
into pure unicameralism.

4. *Two-party system.* Two large parties are in virtually complete control of the party system, and only these two have formed
cabinets since 1935: the Labour party (1935–49, 1957–60, and
1072–75) and the National party (1949–57, 1900–72, and from
1975 on). Moreover, in the thirteen parliamentary elections since
the Second World War, only one other party has been able to win
seats: the Social Credit party won one seat in the general elections of 1966 and 1978, and two in 1981.

5. *One-dimensional party system.* The ethnic cleavage between the white New Zealanders and the indigenous Maoris makes
it impossible to regard New Zealand as an almost completely

16. Stephen Levine, *The New Zealand Political System: Politics in a Small
Society* (Sydney: George Allen and Unwin, 1979), pp. 25–26.

homogeneous society. But the Maori minority is very small and the rest of the population is quite homogeneous. Hence it is not surprising that party politics revolves around socioeconomic issues—Labour representing left-of-center and the National party right-of-center political preferences.

6. Plurality system of elections. New Zealand's unicameral parliament is elected according to the plurality method in single-member districts. The only unusual feature is that there are four special large districts, geographically overlapping the regular smaller districts, that are reserved for Maoris. These four districts entail a deviation from the majoritarianism of the Westminster model because their aim is to guarantee minority representation. Since 1975, Maori voters have had the option to register and vote either in the regular district or in the special Maori district in which they reside.[17] It is not likely that the single-member district plurality system will be changed in the near future, although the severely disproportional results it has produced in recent elections, especially in 1978, have increased public interest in proportional representation: the National party won a clear majority of 51 out of 92 seats in 1978 in spite of the fact that it won neither a majority of the popular vote—its support was only 39.8 percent—nor a plurality, because Labour's popular vote was 40.4 percent. Social Credit's 17.1 percent of the vote yielded only one seat.

7. Unitary and centralized government. The "Act to grant a Representative Constitution to the Colony of New Zealand," passed by the United Kingdom parliament in 1852, created six provinces with considerable autonomous powers and functions vis-à-vis the central government, but these provinces were abol-

17. Alan D. McRobie, "Ethnic Representation: The New Zealand Experience," in Stephen Levine, ed., *Politics in New Zealand: A Reader* (Sydney: George Allen and Unwin, 1978), pp. 270–83.

ished in 1875. Today's governmental system is unitary and centralized.

8. Unwritten constitution and parliamentary sovereignty. Like the United Kingdom, New Zealand lacks a single written constitutional document. Its "unwritten" constitution consists of the Constitution Act of 1952, other basic laws, conventions, and customs. Hence, like the British parliament, the parliament of New Zealand is sovereign. As one of New Zealand's constitutional law experts puts it, "the central principle of the Constitution is that there are no effective legal limitations on what Parliament may enact by the ordinary legislative process."[18]

9. Representative democracy. New Zealand's democracy is mainly representative, but it has also made rather frequent use of the direct democracy device of referendums. Several of these have been concerned with more or less peripheral questions such as liquor licensing, but others have decided centrally important issues: in a 1949 referendum the electorate voted in favor of compulsory military service, and in 1967 they decided to retain the three-year parliamentary term instead of extending it to four years.

In nearly all respects, democracy in New Zealand is more clearly majoritarian, and hence a better example of the Westminster model, than British democracy. Rose even writes that New Zealand is "the only example of the true British system left."[19] There are only two exceptions: the parliamentary seats reserved for the Maori minority and the greater frequency of referendums. However, the former is only a relatively minor deviation from the model, and as far as the latter is concerned, a comparison of

18. K. J. Scott, *The New Zealand Constitution* (Oxford: Clarendon Press, 1962), p. 39.
19. Personal Communication, April 8, 1982.

the Westminster and consensus models shows that exclusively representative government is a less distinctive and less essential feature of the Westminster model than the other eight characteristics—as we shall see in the course of the discussion of the consensus model in the next chapter.

The Consensus Model of Democracy 2

CONSENSUS VS. MAJORITY RULE

The majoritarian interpretation of the basic definition of democracy is that it means "government by the *majority* of the people." It argues that majorities should govern and that minorities should oppose. This view is challenged by the consensus model of democracy. As the Nobel Prize-winning economist Sir Arthur Lewis has forcefully pointed out, majority rule and the government-versus-opposition pattern of government that it implies may be interpreted as undemocratic because they are principles of exclusion. Lewis states that the primary meaning of democracy is that "all who are affected by a decision should have the chance to participate in making that decision, either directly or through chosen representatives." Its secondary meaning is that "the will of the majority shall prevail." If this means that winning parties may make all the governmental decisions and that the losers may criticize but not govern, Lewis argues, the two meanings are incompatible: "to exclude the losing groups from participation in decision-making clearly violates the primary meaning of democracy."[1]

There are two situations in which democracy and majority

1. W. Arthur Lewis, *Politics in West Africa* (London: George Allen and Unwin, 1965), pp. 64–65.

21

rule are not completely incompatible. First, the exclusion of the minority is mitigated if majorities and minorities alternate in government—that is, if today's minority can become the majority in the next election instead of being condemned to permanent opposition. This is how the British and New Zealand two-party systems work. Of course, in these two countries there have also been relatively long periods in which one of the two main parties was kept out of power: the British Labour party for thirteen years (1951–64), the New Zealand National party for fourteen years (1935–49), and New Zealand Labour for twelve years (1960–72).

Even during these extended periods of exclusion from power, one can plausibly argue that democracy and majority rule were not in conflict because of the presence of a second condition: the facts that Britain and New Zealand are relatively homogeneous societies and that their major parties have usually not been very far apart in their policy outlooks because they have tended to stay close to the political center. One party's exclusion from power may be undemocratic in terms of the "government *by* the people" criterion, but if its voters' interests and preferences are reasonably well served by the other party's policies in government, the system approximates the "government *for* the people" definition of democracy.

In less homogeneous societies neither condition applies. The policies advocated by the principal parties tend to diverge to a greater extent, and the voters' loyalties are frequently more rigid, reducing the chances that the main parties will alternate in exercising governmental power. Especially in *plural societies*—societies that are sharply divided along religious, ideological, linguistic, cultural, ethnic, or racial lines into virtually separate subsocieties with their own political parties, interest groups, and media of communication—the flexibility necessary for majoritarian democracy is absent. Under these conditions, majority rule is not only undemocratic but also dangerous, because minorities that are continually denied access to power will feel excluded and discriminated against and will lose their allegiance to the regime. For instance, in the plural society of Northern Ireland, divided into a Protestant majority and a Catholic minority, majority rule meant that the Unionist party representing the Protestant majority won all the elections and formed all of the governments between 1921 and 1972. Massive Catholic protests in the late 1960s developed into a Protestant-Catholic civil war which could only be kept under control by British military intervention and the imposition of direct rule from London.

In plural societies, therefore, majority rule spells majority dictatorship and civil strife rather than democracy. What these societies need is a democratic regime that emphasizes consensus instead of opposition, that includes rather than excludes, and that tries to maximize the size of the ruling majority instead of being satisfied with a bare majority: consensus democracy.

THE CONSENSUS MODEL: EIGHT MAJORITY-RESTRAINING ELEMENTS

The consensus model of democracy may be described in terms of eight elements which stand in sharp contrast to the majoritarian characteristics of the Westminster model. Switzerland and Belgium will serve as our illustrative examples. In the previous chapter, we saw that Great Britain and New Zealand are good but not perfect illustrations of the Westminster model. The same caution must be applied to the Belgian and Swiss cases: they exemplify the consensus model very well, but not perfectly.

1. Executive power-sharing: grand coalitions. In contrast to the Westminster model's tendency to concentrate executive power in one-party and bare-majority cabinets, the consensus principle is to let all of the important parties share executive power in a broad coalition. The Swiss seven-member national executive, the Federal Council, offers an excellent example of such a grand coalition: the three large parties—Christian Democrats, Social Democrats, and Free Democrats—each of which has about one-fourth of the seats in the lower house of the legislature, and the Swiss People's party with about one-eighth of the seats, share the seven executive positions proportionately according to the so-called magic formula of 2 : 2 : 2 : 1, established in 1959. An additional criterion is that the linguistic groups be represented in rough proportion to their sizes: four or five German-speakers, one or two French-speakers, and frequently an Italian-speaker. Both of these criteria are informal rules, but they are strictly obeyed.

The Belgian constitution offers an example of a formal requirement that the executive include representatives of the large linguistic groups. For many years, it had already been the custom to form cabinets with approximately equal numbers of ministers representing the Dutch-speaking majority and the French-speaking minority. One of the constitutional amendments adopted in 1970 made this into a formal rule: "With the possible exception of the Prime Minister, the Cabinet comprises an equal number of French-speaking and Dutch-speaking Ministers."[2] Such a rule does not apply to the partisan composition of the cabinet, although since 1954 all Belgian cabinets have been coalitions of two or more parties with more than merely a bare majority of legislative seats.

2. Separation of powers, formal and informal. The relationship between the executive and the legislature in Switzerland resembles the American presidential pattern rather than the British parliamentary system. The Swiss political scientist Jürg Steiner argues that although the Federal Council is elected by the legislature, it is subsequently invulnerable to legislative attacks: "The members of the council are elected individually for a fixed term of four years, and, according to the Constitution, the

2. Article 86B.

legislature cannot stage a vote of no confidence during that period. If a government proposal is defeated by Parliament, it is not necessary for either the member sponsoring this proposal or the Federal Council as a body to resign."[3] This formal separation of powers makes both the executive and the legislature more independent, and their relationship is much more balanced than the cabinet–parliament relations in Britain and New Zealand, in which the cabinet is clearly dominant. The Swiss Federal Council is powerful but not supreme.

Belgium has a parliamentary form of government with a cabinet dependent on the confidence of the legislature, as in Britain. Nevertheless, Belgian cabinets, largely because they are often broad and uncohesive coalitions, are not at all as dominant as their British counterparts, and they tend to have a genuine give-and-take relationship with parliament. Belgian ministers do not have to be, although they usually are, members of the legislature. The fact that Belgian cabinets are often short-lived attests to their relatively weak position: during the decade of the 1970s, the cabinets were led by five different prime ministers. Although Belgium has a parliamentary system without a formal separation of powers, its executive–legislative relationship may be regarded as an informal or semiseparation of powers.

3. *Balanced bicameralism and minority representation.* The principal justification for instituting a bicameral instead of a unicameral legislature is to give special representation to certain minorities in the second chamber or upper house. Two conditions have to be fulfilled if this minority representation is to be meaningful: the upper house has to be elected on a different basis than the lower house, and it must have real power—ideally, as much power as the lower house. Both of these conditions

3. Jürg Steiner, *Amicable Agreement versus Majority Rule: Conflict Resolution in Switzerland* (Chapel Hill: University of North Carolina Press, 1974), p. 43.

are met in the Swiss system: the National Council is the lower house and represents the Swiss people, and the Council of States is the upper or federal chamber representing the cantons on an equal basis. Hence the small cantons are much more strongly represented in the latter than in the former. Moreover, their respective powers can be summarized as follows: "As a general rule, they have the same rights and duties; neither is superior to the other."[4] Swiss bicameralism is eminently balanced and symmetrical.

The two Belgian chambers of parliament—the Chamber of Representatives and the Senate—also have virtually equal powers. A minority of the senators are indirectly elected by the provincial councils, or coopted, but on the whole the composition of the Senate and the House do not differ a great deal. It is likely, however, that the next stage of constitutional reform in Belgium will overhaul the Senate completely and make it into the representative organ for the linguistic communities and the regions.

4. Multiparty system. Both Switzerland and Belgium have multiparty systems without any party that comes close to majority status. In the 1979 elections to the Swiss National Council, fifteen parties won seats, but the bulk of these seats—169 out of 200—were captured by the four major parties represented on the Federal Council. Switzerland may therefore be said to have a four-party system.

Until the middle of the 1960s, Belgium was characterized by a three-party system consisting of two large parties—Christian Democrats and Socialists—and the medium-sized Liberals. Since then, however, these major parties have split along linguistic lines and a few new linguistic parties have attained prominence, creating at least an eight-party system. This count only includes the "important" parties; in the 1978 and 1981 elections, about a dozen parties won seats in the Chamber of Representatives.

4. George Arthur Codding, Jr., *The Federal Government of Switzerland* (Boston: Houghton Mifflin, 1961), p. 72.

5. Multidimensional party system. The emergence of multiparty systems in Switzerland and Belgium can be explained in terms of two factors. The first is that, unlike Britain and New Zealand, Switzerland and Belgium are plural societies, divided along several lines of cleavage. This multiplicity of cleavages is reflected in the multidimensional character of their party systems. In Switzerland, the religious cleavage divides the Christian Democrats, mainly supported by practicing Catholics, from the Social Democrats and Free Democrats, who draw most of their support from Catholics who rarely or never attend church and from Protestants. The socioeconomic cleavage further divides the Social Democrats, backed mainly by the working class, from the Free Democrats, who have more middle-class support. The Swiss People's party is especially strong among Protestant farmers. The third source of cleavage, language, does not cause much further division in the Swiss party system, although the three large parties are relatively loose alliances of cantonal parties and the linguistic cleavage is a significant differentiator *within* these parties.[5]

Similarly, the religious cleavage in Catholic Belgium divides the Christian Social parties, representing the more faithful Catholics, from the Socialists and Liberals, representing rarely practicing or nonpracticing Catholics. The Socialists and Liberals are divided from each other by class differences. In contrast with Switzerland, the linguistic cleavage in Belgium has caused further splits both by dividing the above three groupings, which used to be Belgium's three dominant parties, into separate and smaller Dutch-speaking and French-speaking parties and by creating a few additional small linguistic parties.[6]

5. Henry H. Kerr, Jr., *Switzerland: Social Cleavages and Partisan Conflict*, Sage Professional Papers in Contemporary Political Sociology, vol. 1, no. 06-002 (London: Sage, 1974), pp. 7–14.

6. André-Paul Frognier, "Party Preference Spaces and Voting Change in Belgium," in Ian Budge, Ivor Crewe, and Dennis Farlie, eds., *Party Identification and Beyond: Representations of Voting and Party Competition* (London: Wiley, 1976), pp. 189–202.

6. Proportional representation. The second explanation for the emergence of multiparty systems in Switzerland and Belgium is that their proportional electoral systems have not inhibited the translation of societal cleavages into party-system cleavages.[7] In contrast with the Westminster model's plurality system, which tends to overrepresent large parties and to underrepresent small parties, the basic aim of proportional representation is to divide the parliamentary seats among the parties in proportion to the votes they receive. The Swiss National Council and both chambers in Belgium are elected by proportional representation.

7. Territorial and nonterritorial federalism and decentralization. Switzerland is a federal state in which power is divided between the central government and twenty-six cantonal governments. Although the central government has become quite powerful, Swiss federalism can still be regarded as decentralized, and the cantons continue to perform a wide range of important tasks. Federalism is the best known, but not the only, method of giving autonomy to different groups in a society. In federal systems, these groups are territorially organized entities: states, cantons, provinces, and so on. Autonomy may also be provided on a nonterritorial basis, and this is of special relevance for plural societies in which the different distinct subsocieties are not geographically concentrated.

Belgium is a good example of nonterritorial "federalism." One of the constitutional amendments adopted in 1970 states: "There is a cultural council for the French cultural community made up of the members of the French linguistic group of both Houses [the Chamber of Representatives and the Senate] and a cultural council for the Dutch cultural community made up of

7. See Gerhard Lehmbruch, *Proporzdemokratie: Politisches System und politische Kultur in der Schweiz und in Österreich* (Tübingen: Mohr, 1967). See also Jürg Steiner, "The Principles of Majority and Proportionality," in Kenneth D. McRae, ed., *Consociational Democracy: Political Accommodation in Segmented Societies* (Toronto: McClelland and Stewart, 1974), pp. 98–106.

the members of the Dutch linguistic group of both Houses."[8] These two cultural councils serve as legislatures with the power to make laws on cultural and educational matters for communities that are only partly defined in territorial terms. The Dutch cultural council legislates for Dutch-speaking Flanders (the Northern part of Belgium excluding Brussels, the capital, which is surrounded by Flemish territory) and for the minority of Dutch-speakers in bilingual Brussels. The French cultural council is the legislature for French-speaking Wallonia (the Southern part of the country) and for the French-speaking majority in Brussels. This arrangement does not fit the definition of conventional territorial federalism, but it is clear that Belgium is no longer a unitary state either. One Belgian constitutional expert suggests that the 1970 constitutional amendments changed the Belgian unitary state into "a communal state."[9]

8. Written constitution and minority veto. Both Belgium and Switzerland have a written constitution: a single document containing the basic rules of governance. Unlike the unwritten constitution of Britain and New Zealand, these written constitutions can only be changed by special majorities. Amendments to the Swiss constitution require the approval in a referendum of not only a nation-wide majority of the voters but also majorities in a majority of the cantons. The latter requirement gives special protection to the smaller cantons, and, when they are united in their opposition to a proposal for constitutional change, it amounts to a minority veto.

The Belgian constitution can only be changed by two-thirds majorities in both chambers of the legislature. This rule also entails a minority veto, if the minority, or a combination of minorites, controls at least a third of the votes in one chamber. More-

8. Article 59B, section 1.
9. Robert Senelle, *The Reform of the Belgian State* (Brussels: Ministry of Foreign Affairs, 1978), p. 139. There is also a cultural council for the tiny German minority in Eastern Belgium.

over, the 1970 constitutional reforms introduced a minority veto on nonconstitutional matters for the purpose of protecting the French-speaking minority against the Dutch-speaking majority. Any bill affecting the cultural autonomy of the linguistic groups requires not only the approval of two-thirds majorities in both chambers but also majorities of each linguistic group—a good example of John C. Calhoun's "concurrent majority" principle. On all other nonfinancial bills, the French-speaking minority in each chamber may appeal to the cabinet, composed of equal numbers of the two language groups, if it feels that its vital interests are threatened.

All of the eight elements of consensus democracy aim at restraining majority rule by requiring or encouraging: the *sharing of power* between the majority and the minority (grand coalitions), the *dispersal of power* (among executive and legislature, two legislative chambers, and several minority parties), a *fair distribution of power* (proportional representation), the *delegation of power* (to territorially or nonterritorially organized groups), and a *formal limit on power* (by means of the minority veto).

DIRECT DEMOCRACY, MAJORITARIANISM, AND CONSENSUS

The ninth characteristic of the Westminster model, discussed in the previous chapter, is a democratic system that is exclusively representative and from which devices of direct democracy, especially the referendum, are absent. Switzerland presents a sharp contrast because it has developed "the theory and practice of the referendum to a pitch which no other nation has begun to match."[10] We should not conclude from this, however, that direct democracy is a characteristic of the consensus model. Our other main examples readily show that this is not the case: majoritar-

10. David Butler and Austin Ranney, "Practice," in David Butler and Austin Ranney, eds., *Referendums: A Comparative Study of Practice and Theory* (Washington, D.C.: American Enterprise Institute, 1978), p. 5.

ian New Zealand uses the referendum fairly frequently, while in consensual Belgium, as in the United Kingdom, only one national referendum has ever been held. Direct democracy is not a distinguishing trait of either the majoritarian or the consensus model. These two models are both models of representative democracy.

It may be argued, of course, that referendums are basically majoritarian in their effects, because they are usually decided by simple popular majorities for or against. They may even be considered more majoritarian than Westminster-style representative democracy, since elected assemblies offer opportunities for minorities to present their case in unhurried discussion and to bargain for support on matters of vital importance to them by promising their adversaries' support on other issues (logrolling). When the voters at large decide an issue, such negotiations are obviously impossible. David Butler and Austin Ranney state: "Because they cannot measure intensities of belief or work things out through discussion and discovery, referendums are bound to be more dangerous than representative assemblies to minority rights."[11]

But the referendum is not invariably a blunt majoritarian instrument. Especially when it is combined with the popular initiative, as in Switzerland, it gives minorities a chance to assert a claim against the wishes of the majority of the elected representatives. A remarkable example of this is a referendum held in Switzerland in 1962 on the initiative of a small party without any representation in either legislative chamber; although all four big parties represented on the Federal Council opposed it, the referendum was successful.[12]

Direct democracy can therefore not be regarded as either typically majoritarian or typically consensual. In fact, it is a foreign element in both majoritarian and consensus democracy be-

11. Butler and Ranney, "Theory," in Butler and Ranney, eds., Referendums, p. 36.
12. Steiner, Amicable Agreement, pp. 18–19.

cause it is the antithesis of representative democracy. On the other hand, elements of direct democracy can be, and have been, introduced in countries which are mainly majoritarian, mainly consensual, or somewhere in between.

INTERMEDIATE FORMS AND PRACTICES: THE CASE OF THE UNITED STATES

Our two basic models of democracy are abstract models of which there are no pure empirical instances, but the four illustrative examples used so far are all close to the end points of the majoritarian-consensual continuum. The other cases of democracy that I shall discuss in this book tend to be further away from the pure models. It is also worth emphasizing again that the position of a particular democratic regime on the continuum is not permanently fixed. As shown in the first chapter, Great Britain was more majoritarian in the 1950s than in the 1970s. Belgium did not become thoroughly consensual until after the passage of the constitutional amendments of 1970, and the Swiss "magic formula" was not adopted until 1959. Similarly, the other democracies tend to move back and forth to some extent on the majoritarian-consensual continuum.

As we shall see in subsequent chapters, the United States is frequently a deviant case among our groups of democracies. However, its place on the continuum is somewhere in the middle. Let us try, as the final topic of this chapter, to describe its position more precisely. In the political science literature there are two divergent traditional interpretations of the basic character of the American democratic system in comparison with other democracies: one emphasizes the similarity of Britain and the United States, placing them in the common category of Anglo-American democracies.[13] The other focuses on the differences between American presidentialism and British parliamentarism, between

13. See, for instance, Gabriel A. Almond, "Comparative Political Systems," *Journal of Politics* 18, no. 3 (August 1956): 391–409.

American federal and British unitary government, between the American loose two-party and the British cohesive two-party system, and so on.[14]

Where does the United States fit on the majoritarian-consensual continuum? In answering this question, we have to keep in mind that the United States can be regarded as a plural society in two respects. First, it is a multiethnic and multiracial society divided into a white majority and black, chicano, and several other smaller minorities. This division is of the greatest contemporary importance. The second line of cleavage, of special significance in the nineteenth and first half of the twentieth centuries, is the regional division between the Northern majority and the Southern minority. As Dahl states, "the South has for nearly two centuries formed a distinctive regional subculture."[15] In terms of the eight differences between the Westminster and consensus models, American democracy can be characterized as follows:

1. Concentration of executive power. The United States is clearly majoritarian in its concentration of executive power in the hands of the president, who is the leader of one of the two main parties and who normally chooses the members of his cabinet from his own party.

2. Separation of powers. One of the best-known and, in comparative perspective, unusual features of American democracy is a formal and strict separation of executive and legislative powers. One of its consequences is that the president, in spite of the concentration of executive power in his hands, is by no means all-powerful. It may even be argued that, although there are no

14. See, for instance, Don K. Price, "The Parliamentary and Presidential Systems," *Public Administration Review* 3, no. 4 (Autumn 1943): 317–34; and William S. Livingston, "Britain and America: The Institutionalization of Accountability," *Journal of Politics* 38, no. 4 (November 1976):879–94.

15. Robert A. Dahl, *Political Oppositions in Western Democracies* (New Haven, Conn.: Yale University Press, 1966), p. 358.

coalition cabinets, a kind of power-sharing between the president and congressional leaders—in particular, for about a century after the Civil War, the leaders of the South who held the chairmanships of key congressional committees—has often been necessary in order to make the most important decisions for the nation.

3. Balanced bicameralism. The House of Representatives and the Senate are examples of legislative chambers with virtually equal powers. Because the states have equal representation in the Senate, the smaller states are more strongly represented there than in the House. This symmetrical bicameral arrangement is identical to that of consensual Switzerland—not surprising, of course, since the United States constitution served as the model for the Swiss federal constitution of 1848 in this respect.

4. Two-party system. A majoritarian characteristic of American democracy is its two-party system, although the Democrats and Republicans hardly resemble the strong, disciplined, and cohesive Labour and Conservative parties in Britain. At the national level, the American parties are at best loose alliances of highly disparate interests.

5. Heterogeneous political parties with similar programs. One of the reasons for the American parties' lack of unity and cohesion is that their social bases are quite heterogeneous but these differences have not been translated into sharply divergent party programs. As chapter 8 will discuss in more detail, only on socioeconomic and cultural-ethnic issues can the main American parties be said to be significantly differentiated: the Democrats have traditionally been the party of the workers and the minorities—including the main groups that can be regarded as minorities in a plural society, the blacks and the South. Compared with most other countries, however, the two issue dimensions of the American party system are not very salient.

6. Plurality system of elections. The typical American electoral method is the plurality single-member-district system (although the two-ballot majority system, multimember districts, and at-large elections are also used, especially at the local level). In recent years, however, two significant deviations in the direction of the consensus model have occurred. One is the Supreme Court's approval of "affirmative gerrymandering": the drawing of electoral district boundaries in such a way as to create black, Puerto Rican, and so on, majorities in these districts and thus to maximize the chances of legislative representation for these groups. Affirmative gerrymandering does not go quite as far as the exclusively Maori districts in New Zealand, but it is similar in its intent. The second major deviation from the plurality method is the change that took place in the 1970s in the method of determining the results of most presidential primaries: from winner-take-all to a more proportional division of the delegates among the presidential candidates according to their share of primary votes.

7. Federalism. The United States has a federal system of the straightforward territorial type. Among other things, it has served the purpose of giving a high degree of autonomy to the South in the American plural society.

8. Written constitution and minority veto. The American written constitution can only be amended by a cumbersome process involving two successive qualified majorities. Another example of the minority veto in American politics is the filibuster in the Senate.

On three or four of the above dimensions, American democracy approximates the majoritarian model (numbers 1, 4, 6, and perhaps 5), and on four, the consensus model (numbers 2, 3, 7, and 8). With regard to the question of direct democracy, the United States is also in an intermediate position: referendums are conducted very frequently in some states, notably California, but the United States is one of very few democracies in which a nationwide referendum has never been held. The concluding chapter of this book will show, however, that there is a clear pattern to these seemingly divergent and contradictory attributes of American democracy: the United States will emerge as the most prominent example of a mixed majoritarian-consensual type of democracy.

Twenty-Two Democratic Regimes 3

THE UNIVERSE OF DEMOCRACIES

Democracy is a recent and rare phenomenon. Not a single democratic government can be found in the nineteenth century, and it was not until the first decade of the twentieth century that in two countries, Australia and New Zealand, fully democratic regimes with firm popular control of governmental institutions and universal adult suffrage were established.[1] Considering the recent origins of modern democracy, its growth in the twentieth century has been spectacular. At the same time, there are still many more of the world's peoples who are governed by nondemocratic than by democratic regimes. Table 3.1 contains a list of the fifty-one countries that could be rated as basically, albeit not perfectly, democratic at the beginning of the 1980s. The ratings are based on two sets of criteria similar to those discussed in chapter 1: political rights, such as the right to participate in free and competitive elections, and civil liberties, such as freedom of speech and association. These fifty-one countries contain roughly 37 percent of the total world population.[2]

1. See Göran Therborn, "The Rule of Capital and the Rise of Democracy," *New Left Review*, no. 103 (May–June 1977), pp. 11–17.
2. Raymond D. Gastil, *Freedom in the World: Political Rights and Civil Liberties 1980* (New York: Freedom House, 1980), pp. 5, 15–24.

TABLE 3.1. The World's Democracies, January 1980

Continuously democratic since about World War II:	Other democratic countries:	
Australia	Bahamas	Nauru
Austria	Barbados	Nigeria
Belgium	Botswana	Papua New Guinea
Canada	Colombia	Portugal
Denmark	Costa Rica	St. Lucia
Finland	Dominica	St. Vincent
France	Dominican Republic	Solomon Islands
West Germany	Ecuador	Spain
Iceland	Fiji	Sri Lanka
Ireland	Gambia	Surinam
Israel	Greece	Trinidad and Tobago
Italy	India	Turkey
Japan	Jamaica	Tuvalu
Luxembourg	Kiribati	Upper Volta
Netherlands	Malta	Venezuela
New Zealand		
Norway		
Sweden		
Switzerland		
United Kingdom		
United States		

Source: Adapted from Raymond D. Gastil. *Freedom in the World: Political Rights and Civil Liberties 1980* (New York: Freedom House, 1980), p. 27.

An additional criterion proposed in chapter 1 in order to determine whether a political system can be called democratic— that is, whether it is sufficiently close to the democratic ideal— is that it must be reasonably responsive to the citizens' wishes over a *long period of time*. For the purpose of this book, we shall operationally define this criterion as the persistence of democratic rule since approximately the end of the Second World War, that is, for at least about thirty to thirty-five years. The advantage of this stringent requirement is that it yields a set of clear and unquestionable cases of democracy on which we can base our comparative analysis.

The application of the continuity criterion to the fifty-one countries in table 3.1 results in the classification of twenty-one of them as continuously democratic since about World War II and thirty as political systems in which democracy was established more recently (in several cases, because independence was not achieved until the 1950s or later) or in which democracy has been seriously interrupted since the late 1940s. Both categories contain a few cases that may raise doubts. Among the long-term democracies, Switzerland is an odd case, because in spite of its long and strong democratic traditions, its female citizens were not granted the right to vote in national elections until 1971. Similarly, the United States does not qualify as a full-fledged democracy until the 1970s, when restrictions on the voting rights of blacks were finally removed as the result of civil rights laws. France is a somewhat doubtful case because its regular democratic processes were briefly suspended during the transition from the parliamentary system of the Fourth Republic to the presidential Fifth Republic. Because of the fundamental differences between these two regimes, France will usually be treated as two distinct cases, the French Fourth Republic and the French Fifth Republic—bringing our total to twenty-one countries and twenty-two democratic regimes.

On the other side of table 3.1, India and Costa Rica are marginal cases. Were it not for the relatively brief but serious interruptions of democratic government in these two countries—by the 1948 civil war in Costa Rica and by the 1975–77 authoritarian interlude in India—both would have been included among the long-term democracies. Most of the other countries have been democratic for only a few years—although the prospects for continued democratic rule may be favorable, such as in Spain and Portugal. On the other hand, three of the democracies, thus classified as of January 1980, were taken over by military coups later in the same year: Turkey, Upper Volta, and Surinam. It should also be pointed out that several of the more recent democracies are so small that they barely qualify as genuinely independent states. Seven have smaller populations than Iceland, the smallest of our long-term democracies with a population of about 225,000; these are Dominica, Kiribati, Nauru, St. Lucia, St. Vincent, the Solomon Islands, and Tuvalu. Nauru and Tuvalu are ministates with populations under 10,000.

Table 3.1 lists only the democracies as of early 1980, and hence it necessarily omits those countries which were democratic during a relatively long period after the Second World War but are no longer so now. The major examples that should be mentioned are Chile, Lebanon, and Uruguay. Lebanese democracy was a good example of the consensus model and could have served well as one of the illustrations of this model in chapter 2, if it had not been thoroughly disrupted in 1975 by a mainly foreign-inspired civil war.

THE TWENTY-ONE LONG-TERM DEMOCRACIES: AN OVERVIEW

Let us now take a closer look at the socioeconomic and cultural characteristics of our key cases of democracy. Several important similarities stand out:

1. All twenty-one countries belong to the well-to-do portion of mankind. There are considerable differences in the gross domestic product (GDP) per capita within our group of countries: in 1980, the Swiss were the most prosperous people, with a per capita GDP about three times that of the Irish and Israelis and more than twice that of the Italians and New Zealanders.[3] But these variations pale in comparison with the differences between this group and most of the countries in the Third World. The per capita GDP figures are widely used as a basic comparative indicator of wealth, but they are not entirely satisfactory because, for the purpose of comparing different countries, their currencies have to be converted to a common currency, usually U.S. dollars,

3. "The OECD Member Countries, 1982 Edition, 18th Year," OECD Observer, no. 115 (March 1982), pp. 26–27.

at the existing exchange rates; the problem is that exchange rates do not necessarily reflect the purchasing power of currencies and they also fluctuate a great deal. A recent study has tried to determine the relative prosperity of thirty-four different countries, including twelve of the long-term democracies, in terms of "international dollars" that express the true purchasing power of the different currencies (as of 1975). Ireland was the "poorest" of our set of democracies: its per capita GDP measured in international dollars was only 42.5 percent of that of the United States. This figure was also somewhat lower than the per capita GDP of three other European countries—Spain, Poland, and Hungary—but higher than that of all eighteen Asian, African, and Latin American countries covered in the study, with the exception of Japan.[4]

2. The high level of economic development of our twenty-one countries is also reflected in their high levels of industrialization and urbanization. Most of the members of the civilian labor force in these countries have industrial and service occupations, and only small numbers are occupied in agriculture, forestry, and fishing: less than 10 percent in the majority of the countries. About three-fourths or more of the people live in urban areas.

3. The twenty-one countries also form a culturally homogeneous group. Twenty belong to the Western Judaeo-Christian cultural world. The only exception is Japan.

4. Most of the twenty-one countries are geographically concentrated in the North Atlantic area: eight continental European countries (France, West Germany, Italy, Switzerland, Austria, the Netherlands, Belgium, and Luxembourg), five Nordic nations (Sweden, Denmark, Norway, Finland, and Iceland), two countries forming the British Isles (the United Kingdom and the Republic of Ireland), and two North American countries (the United

4. Irving B. Kravis, Alan Heston, and Robert Summers, *World Product and Income: International Comparisons of Real Gross Product,* United Nations International Comparison Project: Phase III (Baltimore: Johns Hopkins University Press, 1982), p. 12.

States and Canada). The four nations outside the North Atlantic area are Japan, Israel, Australia, and New Zealand.

An overview of our twenty-one countries also reveals several salient differences among them:

1. There are huge differences in the sizes of the populations, territories, and economies of these countries. The United States is about a thousand times more populous than Iceland, and the United States and Japan together have about the same population as the other nineteen countries combined. The differences in the sizes of their economies are of the same order of magnitude. They differ even more in the extent of their territories: the largest, Canada, is approximately four thousand times as large as Luxembourg. The population density varies from more than three hundred persons per square kilometer in the Netherlands, Belgium, and Japan to two persons per square kilometer in Australia, Canada, and Iceland.

2. There are also major differences in the degree of societal homogeneity or heterogeneity. This factor is of particular importance and interest for our study because it affects the type of democracy—majoritarian, consensual, or mixed—that suits the different countries best. Table 3.2 presents a classification in terms of religious and linguistic differences. A country is classified as "homogeneous" if 80 percent or more of its population belong to the same religion (Roman Catholicism, the different branches of Protestantism combined, Judaism, or the overlapping Buddhist-Shintoist faiths of Japan) or speak the same language. Only three countries are linguistically divided according to this criterion: Belgium, Canada, and Switzerland. There are six religiously divided countries, four of which have approximate Catholic and Protestant parity (Canada, West Germany, the Netherlands, and Switzerland) and two of which have clear Protestant majorities (Australia and the United States). Canada and Switzerland are heterogeneous in both dimensions. The most striking conclusion to be drawn from table 3.2, however, is that two-thirds of our twenty-one countries are quite homogeneous. This is to some

TABLE 3.2.   Extent of Pluralism and Religious-Linguistic
Homogeneity in 21 Democratic Countries

	Nonplural society	Semiplural society	Plural Society
Religiously and linguistically homogeneous	Denmark Iceland Ireland Japan New Zealand Norway Sweden United Kingdom	Finland France Italy	Austria Israel Luxembourg
Religiously and/or linguistically heterogeneous	Australia	Canada Germany United States	Belgium Netherlands Switzerland

Note: "Homogeneous" means that 80 percent or more of the population belongs to the same religious group (Roman Catholics, Protestants, etc.) and linguistic group.

Source: Adapted from Val R. Lorwin, "Segmented Pluralism: Ideological
Cleavages and Political Cohesion in the Smaller European Democracies," Comparative Politics 3, no. 2 (January 1971):148; and Kenneth D. McRae, "Consocia-
tionalism and the Canadian Political System," in Kenneth D. McRae, ed., Consociational Democracy: Political Accommodation in Segmented Societies (Toronto:
McClelland and Stewart, 1974), p. 246.

extent an artifact of our rather lax 80 percent criterion, but rais-
ing the criterion to 90 percent would add only a couple of religiously heterogeneous countries (the United Kingdom and New
Zealand) and no linguistically divided states: the next candidate
for inclusion in the latter category would be Finland, but its
Swedish-speaking minority comprises only about 6 percent of
the population.

3. The more serious weakness of the above classification is
that it masks the degree to which the different countries are plural societies. It fails to indicate whether the religious and linguistic differences—and possibly also other differences such as ideology and race—actually divide the societies into more or less
separate subsocieties with their own political, socioeconomic,

cultural, educational, and recreational organizations. Therefore, table 3.2 also presents a rough threefold categorization of the twenty-one countries into plural, semiplural, and nonplural societies. Among the religiously and linguistically homogeneous countries, six can be regarded as plural or semiplural societies. The explanation is that in the four countries that are overwhelmingly Catholic (Austria, Luxembourg, France, and Italy), there is a politically significant split along religious lines between faithfully practicing Catholics and Catholics who do not attend church regularly or who are Catholic in name only. This cleavage has led to separate networks of Catholic and secular parties and other organizations. Within the secular category, a further split has generally developed between Socialist and Liberal parties and organizations along ideological and class lines. Moreover, in France and Italy there is an especially sharp split between Communists and non-Communists. The same division is present in Finland, which is the third European country with a large Communist party (garnering about 20 percent of the popular vote in the postwar period). In Israel, the cleavages occur between religious and secular Jews and, within the secular camp, between Socialists and Liberals.

Six of the seven religiously and/or linguistically heterogeneous countries can be classified as plural or semiplural societies; Australia is a marginal case, but it is included among the nonplural societies here. Linguistic differences have a strong tendency to divide a society into subsocieties with separate organizational networks, because a common language is a prerequisite for many organizational activities, such as education, the press, radio and television. If our judgment were based solely on the extent of religious and ideological pluralism, Switzerland and Canada would be classified as semiplural and nonplural respectively, but the effect of their linguistic cleavages is to move them into the next more highly plural category.

Nine countries are rated as nonplural in table 3.2 With the exception of Ireland and Japan, all are mainly Protestant. Ireland is the only overwhelmingly Catholic country without a division between practicing and nominal Catholics—mainly because the level of religious practice among all Catholics is very high—and hence without separate religious and secular organizational networks.

Although religious and linguistic homogeneity does not necessarily entail a low degree of pluralism, there is clearly a relationship between the two: the homogeneous countries are much less likely to be plural societies than the heterogeneous ones. It is somewhat surprising that there is no clear relationship between the extent of homogeneity-heterogeneity and pluralism, on the one hand, and the other respect in which the twenty-one countries differ a great deal—size—on the other hand. A plausible hypothesis would be to expect relatively more pluralism in the countries with the larger populations. We see from table 3.2, however, that the larger countries tend to be in the intermediate category of semiplural societies, and that the smaller countries tend to fall into either the plural or nonplural categories.

Subsequent chapters will relate the extent of pluralism in our democratic countries to their form of democracy. Although the relationships are far from perfect, plural societies do tend to show more consensual characteristics than nonplural societies.

4 Executive Power: Majority Rule vs. Power-Sharing

The first and most important difference between the Westminster (majoritarian) and consensus models of democracy concerns the breadth of participation in government, especially the executive branch, by the people's representatives. The Westminster model concentrates executive power in a government supported by a relatively narrow parliamentary majority, whereas the consensus model favors broad coalitions in which all significant political parties and representatives of the major groups in society share executive power (see chapters 1 and 2). Bare-majority and grand coalition governments are the ideal types but, in practice, various intermediate forms can be found, such as broad but not grand coalitions and minority cabinets.

This chapter will explore these different patterns of exercising executive power. It will discuss the major coalition theories, subject them to a critique, and make suggestions for their improvement. The last part of the chapter will be devoted to a review of the empirical findings concerning the types of cabinets which occur in our set of countries that have been continuously democratic since about the Second World War.

COALITION THEORIES

In parliamentary systems of government, cabinets have to be formed in such a way that they will enjoy the confidence of a parliamentary majority. Can we predict which particular cabinet will form if we know the strengths of the different parties in parliament? If one party has a majority of the parliamentary seats, a prediction appears to be easy: the majority party is likely to form a one-party cabinet. It is also possible, however, that it will form a coalition with one or more minority parties; for instance, the British Conservatives had a clear majority in the House of Commons during the Second World War, but Churchill's war cabinet was a grand coalition of the Conservative, Labour, and Liberal parties. If no party has a parliamentary majority, it is likely that a coalition cabinet will be formed, but which coalition is the most likely one? Several theories have been proposed for the purpose of predicting which coalitions will form in parliamentary systems. The five most important of these coalition theories predict the following kinds of coalitions:

1. Minimal winning coalitions (size principle). William H. Riker's size principle predicts that minimal winning coalitions will be formed: coalitions of two or more parties which are winning in the sense that together they control a majority of parliamentary seats, but which are "minimal" in the sense that they will not include any party which is not necessary in order to reach a majority.[1] Figure 4.1 presents an example. Coalition ABC (a cabinet coalition of parties A, B, and C) is a winning coalition because A, B, and C control a majority of 55 out of 100 parliamentary seats. It is minimal because all three parties are necessary in order to form a majority; the elimination of the smallest coalition partner, party A, would reduce the coalition's parliamentary support from a majority of the seats, 55, to a minority of

1. William H. Riker, *The Theory of Political Coalitions* (New Haven, Conn.: Yale University Press, 1962), pp. 32–46.

FIGURE 4.1. Cabinet Coalitions Predicted by Five Coalition
Theories for a Hypothetical Distribution of
Parliamentary Seats

Parties:	A	B	C	D	E	Total
	(Left)				(Right)	
Seats:	8	21	26	12	33	100

Theories:					
Minimal winning coalition	ABC	ADE	BCD	BE	CE
Minimum size		ADE			
Bargaining proposition				BE	CE
Minimal range	ABC		BCD		CE
Minimal connected winning	ABC		BCD		CDE

only 47. The addition of party D to the coalition would make it larger than minimal, because in coalition ABCD either A or D could be eliminated without losing majority support. Minimal winning cabinets may also be called minimal-majority or bare-majority cabinets.

The basic assumption of minimal winning coalition theory is both simple and quite plausible: political parties are interested in maximizing their power. In parliamentary systems, power means participation in the cabinet, and maximum power means holding as many of the cabinet positions as possible. In order to enter the cabinet, a minority party will have to team up with one or more other parties, but it will resist the inclusion of unnecessary parties in the coalition because this would reduce its share of ministers in the cabinet. For instance, in cabinet coalition CE in figure 4.1, party C contributes almost half of the parliamentary support, and hence it is likely to receive almost half of the ministerial appointments. If party B were added to the coalition, C's share of cabinet positions would probably be only a third.

A weakness of minimal winning coalition theory is that it usually does not predict the formation of one particular coalition but instead a range of quite different coalitions all likely to be formed. Only when there is a majority party in parliament can the theory make a single specific prediction: the one minimal winning cabinet that is predicted in this case is a one-party, non-coalition cabinet formed by the majority party. When there is no majority party, minimal winning coalition theory always predicts more than one outcome. In the example of figure 4.1, five different coalitions are predicted.

2. Minimum size coalitions. The second, third, and fourth coalition theories to be discussed here attempt to improve minimal winning coalition theory by introducing additional criteria in order to arrive at more specific predictions. Minimum size coalition theory is based on the same assumption of power maximization as minimal winning coalition theory, but it follows this rationale to its logical conclusion. If political parties want to exclude unnecessary partners from a coalition cabinet in order to maximize their own share of cabinet power, they should also be expected to prefer the cabinet to be based on the narrowest possible parliamentary majority. For instance, it is more advantageous for party E to form coalition ADE with 53 seats than CE with 59 seats. In the former, E's 33 seats in parliament contribute 62 percent of the cabinet's parliamentary support, and in the latter only 56 percent. In a cabinet with twenty ministers, this difference is easily worth an additional ministerial appointment for party E. According to this reasoning, cabinets of minimum size are predicted. In the example of Figure 4.1, coalition ADE with 53 parliamentary seats is predicted rather than the other four coalitions whose sizes range from 54 to 59 seats.

3. Coalitions with the smallest number of parties (bargaining proposition). A different criterion that may be used to choose among the many coalitions predicted by minimal winning coalition theory is Michael Leiserson's "bargaining proposition." He argues that those minimal winning coalitions will tend to form that involve the smallest possible number of parties, because "negotiations and bargaining [about the formation of a coalition] are easier to complete, and a coalition is easier to hold together, other things being equal, with fewer parties."[2] Out of the five minimal winning coalitions in figure 4.1, the bargaining proposition predicts that coalitions BE or CE will form, because they involve only two parties, rather than one of the three-party coalitions.

4. Minimal range coalitions. The preceding theories base their predictions on the sizes and numbers of political parties but ignore their programs and policy preferences. Minimal range coalition theory makes the plausible assumption that it is easier to form and maintain coalitions among parties with similar policy preferences than among parties that are far apart in this respect. Of the several slightly different versions of this theory, figure 4.1 presents the most basic one: the parties are placed on a left–right scale, with party A at the extreme left and E at the extreme right, and the distance between them is measured in terms of the number of "spaces" separating them. The five minimal winning coalitions have ranges of two, three, and four "spaces." If parties seek to form coalitions with like-minded partners, coalition ABC, with a range of two "spaces," is much more likely than coalition ADE, with a range of four "spaces" covering the entire left–right spectrum. Minimal range theory also predicts coalitions BCD and CE, which have the same minimal range of two "spaces" as ABC.

5. Minimal connected winning coalitions. A closely related theory has been proposed by Robert Axelrod.[3] He predicts that coalitions will form that are both "connected"—that is, composed of parties that are adjacent on the policy scale—and devoid of unnecessary partners. The underlying assumption of

2. Michael Leiserson, "Coalition Government in Japan," in Sven Groennings, E. W. Kelley, and Michael Leiserson, eds., The Study of Coalition Behavior: Theoretical Perspectives and Cases from Four Continents (New York: Holt, Rinehart, and Winston, 1970), p. 90.

3. Robert Axelrod, Conflict of Interest: A Theory of Divergent Goals with Applications to Politics (Chicago: Markham, 1970), pp. 165–87.

this theory is that parties will try to coalesce with their immediate neighbors and that other adjacent parties will be added until a majority coalition is formed. The example of figure 4.1 shows that minimal *connected* winning coalitions are not necessarily minimal winning coalitions. According to the latter theory, coalition CDE contains a superfluous partner—party D—but in Axelrod's theory party D is necessary in order to make the coalition a connected one.

The five coalition theories are based on divergent assumptions, and hence they frequently predict different outcomes. In figure 4.1, each theory predicts a set of coalitions that overlaps but is not identical with the sets of coalitions predicted by any other theory. Which of the theories performs best? There have been two major attempts to test the five theories in a large number of countries. Michael Taylor and Michael Laver investigated the cabinet coalitions in twelve continental European countries between 1945 and 1971, and Abram De Swaan analyzed the coalitions in a partly overlapping smaller set of countries (eight European democracies and Israel) but during longer periods, from about 1918 to 1972, in most cases. The aim of both studies was to determine how well the coalition theories were able to predict the actual coalitions that were formed—that is, how much better their predictions were than random guesses—discounting the greater chance that some of the theories have to predict the correct outcome simply because they yield many predictions for any one given parliamentary situation.

Although the two studies used not only different data but also different methods and definitions, their findings are remarkably similar, as table 4.1 shows. Both studies found Axelrod's minimal connected winning theory to be the best predictor; according to De Swaan, "the odds for a random guesser to do better

4. Abram De Swaan, *Coalition Theories and Cabinet Formations: A Study of Formal Theories of Coalition Formation Applied to Nine European Parliaments after 1918* (Amsterdam: Elsevier, 1973), p. 153.

TABLE 4.1. Rank Orders of Predictive Ability of Five Coalition
Theories according to the Taylor-Laver and De
Swaan Studies

Theories	Taylor-Laver	De Swaan
Minimal winning coalition	2	3
Minimum size coalition	5	4.5
Bargaining proposition	4	4.5
Minimal range coalition	3	2
Minimal connected winning coalition	1	1

Source: Based on Michael Taylor and Michael Laver, "Government Coalitions in Western Europe," *European Journal of Political Research* 1, no. 3 (September 1973): 222–27; and Abram De Swaan, *Coalition Theories and Cabinet Formations: A Study of Formal Theories of Coalition Formation Applied to Nine European Parliaments after 1918* (Amsterdam: Elsevier, 1973), pp. 147–58.

are one in five hundred."[4] De Swaan's research also shows that minimal range theory is a reasonably good predictor, but the other three theories do not perform better than completely random predictors.[5] In the Taylor-Laver study, minimal winning theory yielded relatively good results—slightly better than those of minimal range theory—but the general conclusion that emerges from table 4.1 is that *the theories based on the parties' policy preferences perform best.*

A CRITIQUE OF THE POLICY-BLIND
COALITION THEORIES

How can we explain the poor predictive abilities of the three coalition theories based solely on the sizes and numbers of political parties—which are, after all, not implausible criteria? And what can we learn from their failure to predict cabinet coalitions satisfactorily?

1. The first lesson is that the parties' policy preferences can-

5. Eric C. Browne also tested these three theories and found them wanting; see his *Coalition Theories: A Logical and Empirical Critique,* Sage Professional Papers in Comparative Politics, vol. 4, no. 01-043 (Beverly Hills, Calif.: Sage, 1973), pp. 22–30.

not be ignored. This means that parties are not pure power maximizers. They want to participate in cabinets not just in order to hold a share of governmental power but also to collaborate with other like-minded parties and to advance particular policies. Further evidence for this conclusion is provided by the complete failure of minimum size coalition theory, which is based on an extreme version of the power maximization principle.

2. A major problem in evaluating the coalition theories is how to define the membership of coalitions. So far, our discussion has assumed that a political party is a member of a cabinet coalition if one or more of its representatives become cabinet ministers. But it is also possible for a party to support a cabinet without entering it. One example, discussed in chapter 2, was the 1977–78 Labour–Liberal coalition in Britain; the Liberals provided support for the Labour cabinet in exchange for consultations on cabinet policy but without placing any Liberals in the cabinet. The Italian Communists had a similar relationship with the Christian Democratic cabinets from 1976 to 1979. These cabinets have been called "grand coalitions," but it is obviously only possible to do so if the Communist party can be regarded as having been a "member" of the coalition on the strength of its support of, but nonparticipation in, the cabinets.[6] One of the differences between the De Swaan and the Taylor-Laver studies, cited earlier, is that the former does and the latter does not consider support parties to be coalition members.

The ambivalent meaning of coalition membership is not only a definitional problem but also has theoretical implications for the policy-blind coalition theories. Support parties violate the assumption that parties are interested mainly in acquiring a share of cabinet power. Instead, the usual reward for support parties is influence on government policy—again demonstrating the importance of policy considerations in coalition formation. Of course,

6. See Luigi Graziano, "The Historic Compromise and Consociational Democracy: Toward a 'New Democracy'?", *International Political Science Review* 1, no. 3 (1980):345–68.

parties may have other motivations for supporting but not entering cabinets: it is an intermediate status which may be regarded as a stepping-stone toward full-fledged cabinet membership— the Italian Communist party's strategy in 1976–79—or an attractive way of having some influence on cabinet policy without having to take full responsibility for it.

3. The assumption that parties want to acquire a maximum share of cabinet power is usually interpreted as implying that they will seek to enter a cabinet whenever a new cabinet has to be formed. However, a party may also decide that it would be electorally advantageous to stay out of the cabinet temporarily in order to gain a stronger position to enter it, and a stronger role in it, after a period of opposition.

4. The assumption of power maximization leads to the prediction that the smallest possible winning coalitions will be formed, but there may be important countervailing pressures that will tend to enlarge coalitions. One explicitly acknowledged by Riker himself is the "information effect": in the negotiations about the formation of a cabinet, there may be considerable uncertainty about how loyal one or more of the prospective coalition parties, or individual legislators belonging to these parties, will be to the proposed cabinet. Therefore, additional parties may be brought into the coalition as insurance against defections and as guarantee for the cabinet's winning status. In Riker's words, "if coalition-makers do not know how much weight a specific uncommitted participant adds, then they may be expected to aim at more than a minimum winning coalition."[7]

5. Another factor that may force the enlargement of coalitions is that "winning" does not always mean merely having a regular parliamentary majority. Since the beginning of the process of fundamental constitutional reform in Belgium around 1970, several efforts have been made to form cabinets based on parties controlling at least two-thirds of the seats in parliament, because

7. Riker, *The Theory of Political Coalitions*, p. 88.

constitutional amendments require approval by two-thirds majorities.

6. Conversely, a cabinet may be "winning" with less than majority support in parliament. This can be achieved not only with the help of steady support parties, as discussed earlier, but also if a cabinet is able to find shifting parliamentary majorities to lend support on votes of confidence and legislative proposals. An example is the Swedish Social Democratic cabinet, which governed alternately with the support of the Communists on the left and the Center party on the right in the early 1960s.

A CRITIQUE OF THE POLICY-BASED COALITION THEORIES

Although the coalition theories that take the parties' policy preferences into account—minimal range and minimal connected winning theory—perform much better than the policy-blind theories, they are by no means perfect and immune to criticism. For one thing, De Swaan found that minimal connected winning theory had outstanding predictive ability compared with random guesses, but that only half of the 108 actual coalitions he studied were of the minimal connected winning type.[8] What are the weaknesses of the policy-based theories?

1. One problem is that the assignment of parties to positions on the left–right scale may involve circular reasoning. Where a party stands on left–right issues may be inferred from its formal program, its votes in parliament, and so on, but these may be determined to a large extent by whether the party is or has been a member of the government and with which other parties it has formed a coalition. In Germany, for instance, the Free Democratic party is now usually assigned a center position on the policy scale—in contrast with the right-of-center position of other

8. De Swaan, *Coalition Theories and Cabinet Formations*, p. 148.

European Liberal parties—because it participated in several cabinet coalitions with the leftist Social Democrats from 1969 to 1982. Explaining these coalitions in terms of the two parties' adjacent policy positions, which are in turn derived from their coalition behavior, obviously does not explain anything. This circular reasoning makes the policy-based theories look stronger than they really are.

2. On the other hand, the policy-based theories are needlessly weakened if they interpret proximity of policy preferences exclusively in terms of the left–right dimension. In most of the continental European states, the religious–secular dimension is also very important, and other policy factors such as ethnic, linguistic, and regional conflict and divergent foreign policy orientations are salient in several countries. For instance, the 1954–58 Socialist–Liberal cabinet in Belgium was neither a minimal range nor a connected coalition, measured on the left–right scale, because it failed to include the Christian Democrats in the center. However, the Socialists and Liberals are both secular parties and hence their coalition was both of minimal range and connected in terms of the religious–secular dimension. Another example is the broad coalition cabinet formed in 1948 in the Netherlands—considerably larger than a minimal winning coalition because it had to deal with the issue of granting independence to Indonesia, which required a two-thirds parliamentary majority—consisting of the Socialists on the left, the Catholic party and the (Protestant) Christian Historical Union in the center, and the Liberals on the right, but not including the Anti-Revolutionaries, the other major centrist Protestant party. This coalition cannot be explained in terms of the left–right dimension, but it was a connected coalition in terms of the all-important colonial policy dimension, because the Anti-Revolutionary party was the only large party advocating a diehard anti-independence policy.

3. It should be remembered that the policy-based theories also take the size principle into account. They represent addi-

tions, instead of alternatives, to minimal winning theory: minimal range coalitions are also minimal winning coalitions, and minimal connected winning coalitions either equal or are only slightly larger than minimal winning size. In reality, however, the parties' policy preferences may exert strong pressure to enlarge instead of to minimize the size and range of coalitions. One reason is that a political party naturally prefers to form a cabinet that will follow policies close to its own policy preferences; a cabinet in which it participates with parties of about equal weight on both its left and its right is ideal in this respect. In the example of figure 4.1 above, if B and C are inclined to participate in a coalition together, coalition ABC is more attractive to B because B occupies the center position in it, whereas for the same reason C prefers coalition BCD. In such a situation, it is not at all unlikely that the oversized coalition ABCD will be formed. Center parties have better opportunities to form balanced coalitions in which they are pivotal than parties near the ends of the policy scale; hence they are especially likely to press for oversized coalitions.[9]

4. Policy considerations also lead to oversized or even grand coalitions if it is the overriding objective of all or most of the parties to work together to defend the country or the democratic regime against external or internal threats. Wars are the main external threats, and wartime grand coalitions, such as Churchill's war cabinet in Britain, have occurred frequently. Internal threats may be posed by antidemocratic parties and movements and by deep differences between prodemocratic parties in plural societies. Moreover, especially in plural societies, the norm of consensus democracy may prescribe that the major prodemocratic parties be allowed to participate in governing as much as

9. De Swaan's own "policy distance theory," which is exclusively based on the assumption that parties will prefer that coalition which is closest to their own policy preference, is not a good predictor of actual cabinet coalitions (ibid., pp. 151–53).

possible. Ian Budge and Valentine Herman tested the following hypothesis in twenty-one countries during the 1945–78 period: "Where the democratic system is immediately threatened (externally or internally), all significant pro-system parties will join the government, excluding anti-system parties." They found that of the cabinets formed under such crisis conditions, 72 percent were indeed grand coalitions.[10]

De Swaan's overall conclusion is that minimal connected winning theory "holds in normal times," that "the tendency to form coalitions of minimal range disappears in times of crisis," but that the tendency to form connected coalitions "remains throughout."[11] In other words, a general characteristic of coalition cabinets is that they are connected coalitions, but their size varies a great deal depending on whether conditions are "normal." In order to discover what is meant by "normal" coalition formation, we shall have to look at the actual patterns of coalitions of different sizes in our set of democracies.

COALITION POTENTIAL AND COALITION PACTS

Before turning to these empirical data on cabinet coalitions, we must consider two additional suggestions to improve the predictive power of coalition theories. These are based on what may be known about the *intentions* of the different parties with regard to coalition formation.

First, one or more parties may lack coalition potential; that is, they may be excluded from the process of coalition formation by the other parties either because they are regarded as antidemocratic or because they are too small to contribute significantly

10. Ian Budge and Valentine Herman, "Coalitions and Government Formation: An Empirically Relevant Theory," *British Journal of Political Science 8,* no. 4 (October 1978):463, 469.
11. De Swaan, *Coalition Theories and Cabinet Formations,* p. 159.

to the parliamentary strength of a coalition. If we make use of this knowledge, we can make more accurate predictions about coalitions. To use the example of figure 4.1 again, let us assume that party A on the extreme left is a Communist party, and that it is an unacceptable coalition partner for the other parties. In that case, coalition ABC cannot be formed, and minimal connected winning theory can narrow its predictions to coalitions BCD and CDE.

Second, it often happens that prior to election day certain parties will indicate that they intend jointly to form a coalition if the electoral outcome is favorable to them. If this applies to parties A, B, and C, which win a majority of 55 out of 100 seats in figure 4.1, then obviously coalition ABC can be predicted. In the 1980 Bundestag elections in Germany, three parties won seats: 218 were won by the Social Democrats on the left, 53 by the centrist Free Democrats, and 226 by the rightist Christian Democrats. Minimal range and minimal connected winning coalition theory would have predicted two possible coalitions: a Social Democratic–Free Democratic and a Free Democratic–Christian Democratic coalition. However, the cabinet in power before the election was a coalition of Social Democrats and Free Democrats led by Chancellor Helmut Schmidt, and these two parties were committed to continue their collaboration if the electorate's verdict would permit it. Based on this information, only a Social Democratic–Free Democratic coalition should have been predicted—and this was the cabinet that was actually formed. Other examples of such pre-election pacts and understandings are: the alliance of the Socialists and Communists, on the one hand, and the alliance of Gaullists, Independents, and Centrists, on the other, in the 1978 elections in France; the enduring and close cooperation of the Liberal and Country parties in Australia; the alliance of the three "bourgeois" (non-Socialist) parties in Sweden in the late 1970s; and the 1977 electoral pact of Socialists and Democrats '66 (a left-of-center party) in the Netherlands.

TYPES OF CABINETS IN TWENTY-ONE DEMOCRACIES: EMPIRICAL FINDINGS

The third, fourth, and fifth columns of table 4.2 show the types of cabinets that have occurred in our set of democracies in terms of the percentage of the time that each type of cabinet was in power from 1945 to 1980 (that is, from the first to the last parliamentary election in each country in the 1945–80 period). Since it is usually difficult, and often completely impossible, to determine which parties are support parties, the table is based on a strict definition of cabinet membership: only the actual participants in cabinets are counted, and support parties, if any, are not considered members of a coalition.[12] Three types are distinguished: minimal winning, oversized (larger than minimal winning), and minority cabinets. Oversized cabinets are, by definition, coalition cabinets, since they contain one or more unnecessary parties, but it should be noted that minimal winning and minority cabinets may be either coalition or single-party cabinets.

In addition to the eighteen parliamentary systems of government among our twenty-two democratic regimes, table 4.2 also includes Finland, the French Fifth Republic, and Switzerland. Finland has a presidential system, but it also has a cabinet dependent on the parliament's confidence. France had a regular parliamentary government until 1958, and in the presidential Fifth Republic from 1958 on there continues to be a cabinet that can be dismissed by parliament. The Swiss seven-member Federal Council is not subject to the parliament's confidence, but it *is* elected by parliament. Only the United States presidential system is so deviant that it cannot be included in this analysis.

The fact that the period covered by table 4.2 begins immediately after the Second World War leads to a slight understatement of oversized cabinets, but nevertheless the twenty-one re-

12. This is also the definition used by Lawrence C. Dodd, *Coalitions in Parliamentary Government* (Princeton, N.J.: Princeton University Press, 1976).

TABLE 4.2. Proportions of Time during which Minimal Winning, Oversized, and Minority Cabinets Were in Power in 21 Democracies, 1945–1980

	Adjusted percentages		Unadjusted percentages		
	Minimal winning cabinets (%)	Oversized cabinets (%)	Minimal winning cabinets (%)	Oversized cabinets (%)	Minority cabinets (%)
New Zealand	100	0	100	0	0
Luxembourg	96	4	96	4	0
United Kingdom	95	5	90	0	10
Ireland	89	11	78	0	22
Iceland	88	12	86	10	4
Canada	87	13	73	0	27
Austria	86	14	84	11	4
Australia	86	14	86	14	0
Norway	83	17	67	0	33
Japan	81	19	77	15	8
Germany	78	22	78	22	0
Belgium	76	24	75	22	3
Denmark	66	34	32	0	68
Sweden	66	34	32	0	68
Finland	38	62	25	50	25
France V	37	63	37	63	0
Italy	35	65	17	46	36
Netherlands	27	73	25	71	4
France IV	20	80	0	60	40
Israel	18	82	17	81	1
Switzerland	0	100	0	100	0
All 21 regimes	67	33	59	25	17

Source: Based on data in Jean-Claude Colliard, *Les Régimes parlementaires contemporains* (Paris: Presses de la Fondation Nationale des Sciences Politiques, 1978), pp. 311–54; Eric C. Browne and John Dreijmanis, eds., *Government Coalitions in Western Democracies* (New York: Longman, 1982); and *Keesing's Contemporary Archives* (London: Keesing's Publications).

gimes together had minimal winning cabinets only 59 percent of the time. The remaining time was divided between oversized cabinets (25 percent) and minority cabinets (17 percent). The most striking feature of the table is the enormous variation in the pattern of cabinet types among the twenty-one democracies. Twelve were governed by minimal winning cabinets most of the time, seven mainly by oversized governments, and two—Denmark and Sweden—by minority cabinets for more than two-thirds of the period.

How can this remarkable variation in types of cabinet be explained? In line with the main theme of this book, minimal winning cabinets are a characteristic of the Westminster model of democracy and can be expected to occur in democracies that approximate the Westminster model and that are homogeneous societies. Oversized cabinets are more typical of the consensus model, and they are particularly suitable for governing plural societies. Of the four examples discussed in chapters 1 and 2, New Zealand and Switzerland fit this pattern perfectly: New Zealand had nothing but minimal winning cabinets, and Switzerland experienced only oversized cabinets. Minority cabinets are more difficult to interpret along these lines. They may be near-majority cabinets which govern with the steady support of one other party that gives them a parliamentary majority. But they may also be either near-majority or much smaller cabinets that govern with the support of shifting parliamentary coalitions. The former resemble minimal winning cabinets, and the latter oversized cabinets. Since we are mainly interested in the contrast between minimal winning and oversized cabinets, the minority cabinet periods are apportioned equally to these two basic types in the adjusted percentages of table 4.2—a realistic and reasonable, albeit rough, approximation.

Table 4.3 classifies the twenty-one regimes according to whether they are plural, semiplural, or nonplural and according to the type of cabinet that they have experienced most frequently (adjusted percentages). There is a relationship between the two

TABLE 4.3. Extent of Pluralism and Usual Types of Cabinets in 21 Democracies, 1945–1980

	Nonplural society	Semiplural society	Plural society
Minimal winning cabinets (More than 85% of the time)	Australia Iceland Ireland New Zealand United Kingdom	Canada	Austria Luxembourg
Minimal winning cabinets (85% of the time or less)	Denmark Japan Norway Sweden	Germany	Belgium
Oversized cabinets		Finland France IV France V Italy	Israel Netherlands Switzerland

variables, but it is not a very strong one. If our hypothesis were entirely correct, all twenty-one democracies would fit on the diagonal of the upper-left, middle, and lower-right cells. Actually, fewer than half of our countries fit this pattern, but the others are only slightly off the diagonal, with the exception of Austria and Luxembourg, which are completely deviant. Belgium also appears to be an embarrassing exception, because it served as one of the prime examples of consensus democracy in chapter 2.

The puzzle can be solved, and our hypothesis can be strengthened, by a closer look at these three deviant cases. Two adjustments to the hypothesis can be derived from the Austrian case. First, minimal winning cabinets may occur in plural societies, but if they do, they may lead to serious tensions and instability. During the period of the First Republic (1918–33), the two major communities in the Austrian plural society, Catholics and Socialists, and the two large parties representing these communities, were extremely antagonistic toward each other. The fact that the Socialists were excluded from the government from 1920 on fueled their mutual suspicion and hostility, eventually leading to civil war and the establishment of a fascist regime. After the Second World War, the leaders of the two parties recognized the dangers of majoritarian government in a plural society, and in order to prevent a repetition of the sorry experience of the First Republic, they embarked on a power-sharing venture that lasted until 1966. This grand coalition turned out to be so successful in alleviating their mutual tensions, that the regime could safely return to majoritarianism: the Catholic People's party formed a one-party cabinet in 1966, with the Socialists in the opposition, and their roles were reversed in 1970.

The second lesson to be learned from the Austrian case is that the definition of minimal wining cabinets can be very misleading: the *grosse Koalition* that ruled Austria from 1945 to 1966 was technically a "minimal winning coalition" during most of this period. In 1945, the People's party won an absolute majority of the seats in the National Council, and its coalition with the Socialists (and, for a while, with the Communists) therefore entailed the inclusion of unnecessary parties; the coalition was clearly oversized. From 1949 to 1966, however, neither large party controlled an absolute majority of the seats and hence neither party was "unnecessary" for the coalition. On the other hand, these two parties' combined strength in parliament exceeded 92 percent of the seats on the average, with the Freedom party and the Communists dividing the rest. It is technically correct but quite unrealistic to call this cabinet a minimal winning instead of a grand coalition.

When we take a closer look at the seemingly deviant case of Belgium, three further lessons emerge. First, we should remember that it is the purpose of power-sharing in a plural society to include all significant subsocieties in decision-making as much as possible. If each subsociety is represented by its own political party, power-sharing normally means oversized or grand multiparty coalition cabinets; but parties and subsocieties do not necessarily correspond closely. In Belgium, the Dutch-speaking and

TABLE 4.4. Proportions of Time during which the Major
Austrian, Belgian, and Luxembourg Parties
Participated in Cabinets, 1945–1980

	Catholic Party (%)	Socialist Party (%)	Liberal Party (%)
Austria	73	88	—
Belgium	84	61	46
Luxembourg	85	55	64

Source: Based on data in Jean-Claude Colliard, *Les Régimes parlementaires contemporains* (Paris: Presses de la Fondation Nationale des Sciences Politiques, 1978), pp. 311–54; Wilfried Dewachter and Edi Clijsters, "Belgium: Political Stability despite Coalition Crises," in Eric C. Browne and John Dreijmanis, ed., *Government Coalitions in Western Democracies* (New York: Longman, 1982), pp. 187–216; and *Keesing's Contemporary Archives* (London: Keesing's Publications).

French-speaking communities are each represented by several parties. It has therefore been possible to form grand coalitions of Dutch-speakers and French-speakers in the cabinet—first as an informal rule, and from 1970 on formally mandated by the constitution—without having grand coalitions of political parties.

Second, grand coalitions may be formed outside of the cabinet. Power-sharing may take the form of permanent or ad hoc "grand" councils and committees that play not much more than an advisory role formally but actually exert great influence. A good example provided by the Belgian case is the extra-cabinet grand coalition of the leaders of the Catholic, Socialist, and Liberal parties that settled the all-important and highly divisive issue of state aid to religious schools in 1958. This grand coalition negotiated the school pact while a minimal winning cabinet of Socialists and Liberals was in power.

Third, the frequency of minimal winning cabinets in Belgium has not entailed the exclusion of any of the three major parties from the cabinet for very long periods. As table 4.4 shows for the postwar years, the same conclusion applies to Luxembourg and Austria. In Belgium and Luxembourg, the Catholic parties are clearly the pivotal coalition partners, but the Socialists and Liberals tend to participate in cabinets about half of the time.

A final comment is in order concerning Canada, although it is only a slightly deviant case in table 4.3. Canadian cabinets tend to be one-party majority or, especially since the Second World War, one-party minority governments. Nevertheless, several of these cabinets can be regarded as grand coalitions of representatives of the two large ethnic-linguistic communities; in particular, the Liberal party has strong support among both English-speakers and French-speakers. Hence, as in the Belgian case, cabinets that are minimal winning—or smaller than minimal winning—in terms of political parties, may be grand coalitions in terms of the major subsocieties in a plural society.

The Canadian case is also instructive because it demonstrates the normative influence of the Westminster model—which is in conflict with Canada's need for consensual institutions and practices to deal with its ethnic-linguistic cleavage. Valentine Herman and John Pope write: "In Canada . . . the conventions of government borrowed so heavily from Britain effectively preclude the formation of coalition governments"; one-party majority cabinets are the ideal, and a one-party minority government is preferred by all the parties and the electorate to a multi-party majority government.[13] Sir Arthur Lewis even compares the Westminster model's bias against coalitions and oversized cabinets to brainwashing, and he suggests that the leaders of plural societies may need "much un-brainwashing" in order to "grasp their problems in true perspective."[14]

13. Valentine Herman and John Pope, "Minority Governments in Western Democracies," *British Journal of Political Science* 3, no. 2 (April 1973):195.

14. W. Arthur Lewis, *Politics in West Africa* (London: Allen and Unwin, 1965), p. 55.

Executive-Legislative Relations: Patterns of Dominance and Balance of Power

5

The second difference between the Westminster and consensus models of democracy concerns the relationship between the executive and legislative branches of government. The majoritarian model is one of executive dominance, whereas the consensus model is characterized by a more balanced executive-legislative relationship. In real political life, a variety of patterns between complete balance and severe imbalance can occur.

This chapter will first contrast the two most prevalent formal arrangements of executive-legislative relations in democratic regimes: parliamentary government and presidential government. It will propose a classificatory scheme based on the two major differences between these types of government, and it will present a critique of the proposition that parliamentarism and presidentialism are distinguished by several other criteria. After a discussion of the relative strengths and weaknesses of parliamentary and presidential systems, the relationship between parliamentarism and presidentialism, on the one hand, and majoritarian and consensus democracy, on the other, will be analyzed. Can executive dominance and executive-legislative balance be linked to the differences between the two formal governmental types? Are the two types equally compatible with majoritarian and consensus democracy?

PARLIAMENTARY VS. PRESIDENTIAL GOVERNMENT

Parliamentary government, or cabinet government, can be concisely defined as "the form of constitutional democracy in which executive authority *emerges from*, and is *responsible to*, legislative authority."[1] The two crucially important characteristics of parliamentary government which distinguish it from presidential government, are italicized in the definition. First, in a parliamentary system, the chief executive—who may have different official titles such as prime minister, premier, chancellor, minister-president, or taoiseach, but to whom we shall generically refer as the prime minister—and his or her cabinet are responsible to the legislature in the sense that they are dependent on the legislature's confidence and that they can be dismissed from office by a legislative vote of no confidence or censure. In a presidential system, the chief executive—the president—is elected for a constitutionally prescribed period and in normal circumstances cannot be forced to resign by a legislative vote of no confidence (although it may be possible to remove a president for criminal wrongdoing by the process of impeachment). Another way of expressing this difference between presidentialism and parliamentarism is to contrast *separation* of the executive and legislative powers with *fusion* of these powers.

The second difference between presidential and parliamentary governments is that presidents are popularly elected, either directly or via an electoral college, and that prime ministers are selected by the legislatures. The process of selection may take a variety of forms. For instance, the West German chancellor, the Irish taoiseach, and the Japanese prime minister are formally elected by the Bundestag, the Dáil, and the Japanese House of Representatives, respectively. In Italy and Belgium, cabinets emerge from negotiations among the parties in parliament and

1. Leon D. Epstein, "Parliamentary Government," in David L. Sills, ed., *International Encyclopedia of the Social Sciences* (New York: Macmillan and Free Press, 1968), 11:419 (italics added).

especially among the party leaders, but they also require a formal parliamentary vote of investiture. In the United Kingdom, the king or queen normally appoints the leader of the majority party to the prime ministership, and in most of the multiparty systems, too, the cabinets that emerge from interparty bargaining are appointed by the heads of state without formal election or investiture; these cabinets are assumed to have the legislature's confidence unless and until it expresses its lack of confidence.

Because parliamentary and presidential governments are defined in terms of two distinctive characteristics, the combination of these traits yields the four possible governmental types shown in the typology of table 5.1. In addition to the pure parliamentary and presidential types, there are two hybrid forms of government. Nineteen of our twenty-two democracies fit the criteria of one of the two pure types without difficulty; the overwhelming majority, eighteen out of twenty-two, are parliamentary systems, and the United States is the sole case of pure presidentialism.

The only example of the first hybrid form is Switzerland: its "cabinet," the Federal Council, is elected by parliament, but the seven councillors stay in office for a fixed four-year term and cannot be dismissed by a legislative vote of no confidence. The United States would have provided another example, if the Constitutional Convention of 1787 had not changed its mind at the last moment; the Virginia plan included the election of the chief executive by the national legislature, and the Convention voted three times in favor of it before finally settling on the electoral college solution. It should also be noted that if no presidential candidate wins a majority in the electoral college, the United States Constitution prescribes the first hybrid form of table 5.1 as the next step: election by the House of Representatives. There are no empirical examples of the second hybrid form of government. As we shall see below, however, an important proposal for the strengthening of presidential government fits this category to a certain extent.

Table 5.1. Parliamentary, Presidential, and Hybrid Forms of Government in 22 Democracies: A Typology

		Chief executive	
		Dependent on the legislature's confidence	Not dependent on the legislature's confidence
Chief executive is selected by the:	Legislature	**Parliamentary Government:** Australia Austria Belgium Canada Denmark France IV Germany Iceland Ireland	Israel Italy Japan Luxembourg Netherlands New Zealand Norway Sweden United Kingdom	**Hybrid Form of Government I:** Switzerland
	Voters	**Hybrid Form of Government II:** No empirical examples	**Presidential Government:** Finland France V United States

Table 5.1 presents one rather serious problem of classification: in which of the categories do we place democratic regimes with two "chief" executives—both a popularly elected president with a fixed term of office and a prime minister selected by and dependent on the legislature? In such cases, we have to ask who is the more powerful of the two: who really is the *chief* executive? The application of this criterion leads to the classification of France and Finland as presidential governments. In the Finnish case, it may also be argued that the president, elected by an electoral college roughly comparable to that of the United States, and the prime minister have approximately equal powers, and hence that Finland has a mixed presidential-parliamentary sys-

tem. In the case of France, there is no doubt at all. The Third Republic (1870–1940) and Fourth Republic (1946–58) were parliamentary governments, but, especially since the adoption of the 1962 constitutional amendment prescribing direct popular election of the president, the Fifth Republic has clearly been a presidential government.[2]

ADDITIONAL PARLIAMENTARY-PRESIDENTIAL CONTRASTS

A few eminent political scientists have argued that in addition to the two crucial differences between parliamentary and presidential systems discussed above, there are several other differences.[3] Upon closer examination, these contrasts turn out to be relatively unimportant and not really essential for the distinction between the two major forms of government.

1. The concept of fusion of power suggests not only that the executive is dependent on the legislature's confidence but also that the same persons are or may be members of both parliament and the cabinet. Similarly, separation of powers, as in the United States, means the independence of the executive and legislative branches as well as the rule that the same person cannot simultaneously serve in both. Most of the democracies classified as parliamentary or presidential in terms of the two crucial characteristics also fit this additional criterion, but there are exceptions. In the United States and France—and also in Switzerland—legislators cannot be members of the executive, but this rule does not apply to the Finnish cabinet. In fifteen of the eigh-

2. Ezra N. Suleiman, "Presidential Government in France," in Richard Rose and Ezra N. Suleiman, eds., *Presidents and Prime Ministers* (Washington, D.C.: American Enterprise Institute, 1980) , pp. 94–138.
3. Douglas V. Verney, *The Analysis of Political Systems* (London: Routledge and Kegan Paul, 1959), pp. 17–56; Ivo D. Duchacek, *Power Maps: Comparative Politics of Constitutions* (Santa Barbara, Calif.: ABC-Clio Press, 1973), pp. 175–91; and Klaus von Beyme, *Die parlamentarischen Regierungssysteme in Europa* (Munich: Piper, 1970), pp. 41–43.

teen parliamentary systems, membership in the cabinet may be combined with membership in parliament, but in Luxembourg, the Netherlands, and Norway they are incompatible. However, in these three countries, cabinet members do participate in parliamentary debates. Because the incompatibility rule emphasizes the separate status of the cabinet, it tends to strengthen the cabinet's authority vis-à-vis parliament, but it cannot be considered more than a minor variation within the parliamentary type. It would certainly be incorrect to argue that Luxembourg, the Netherlands, and Norway fit or even approximate the presidential form of government in this respect.

2. A logical corollary of the legislature's power to dismiss the cabinet in a parliamentary system is the prime minister's right to dissolve parliament and call new elections. In a presidential system, similarly, the inability of the legislature to dismiss the president is matched by the president's inability to dissolve the legislature. Again, most of our twenty-two democratic regimes fulfill this condition, but in the French presidential system as well as in Finland, parliament can be dissolved by the executive, whereas in the Norwegian parliamentary system the executive does not have this right. Moreover, the executive's right to dissolve the legislature was present in only a very weak form in the otherwise clearly parliamentary Fourth French Republic. Executive authority is obviously affected by whether it does or does not have such power over the legislature, but this factor cannot be considered an essential distinction between parliamentarism and presidentialism.

3. There are two further distinctions that fit all of our empirical cases without exception, but which have to do with more or less accidental rather than necessary attributes of the different types of government. All of our parliamentary governments have divided executives: a symbolic and ceremonial head of state (a monarch or president) who has little power, and a prime minister who is the head of the government and who, together with the cabinet, exercises most executive power. In presidential sys-

tems, the president is simultaneously the head of state and the head of the government. The President of the United States provides the best example, but the French president, too, is not only the head of state but also the real head of the government; the prime minister is merely the president's principal adviser and assistant. Finland may be regarded as a partial exception because its prime minister shares governmental power with the president on a coequal, or nearly equal, basis.

It is not at all clear, however, that a dual executive is an essential ingredient of parliamentarism and that a single chief executive is a necessary attribute of presidentialism. In parliamentary systems, the head of state usually has the formal duty to appoint the head of government. But the real selection of the prime minister and his cabinet is performed by the party leaders in parliament, and election by parliament can easily be substituted for appointment by the head of state. The other ceremonial and symbolic functions can be exercised by the head of the government. In short, it should be possible for a prime minister to be the head of both the government and the state in parliamentary systems. Most of the *Länder* (states) of the West German and Austrian federal republics have such parliamentary governments without a separate head of state. Conversely, it should be possible for presidential systems to have a dual executive. For instance, there was a great deal of public debate in the Netherlands in the late 1960s and early 1970s about a proposal to have the prime minister elected directly by the voters for a four-year term but not to change the monarchy. In effect, such a "prime minister" would be the head of the government in a presidential system—but not the head of state, because the monarch would continue in that position.

4. The final difference between parliamentary and presidential systems that is frequently mentioned in the scholarly literature is that the president is the sole executive whereas the prime minister and the cabinet form a collective executive body. This characterization fits our cases well, although, in the parliamen-

tary systems, the position of the prime minister in the cabinet varies between one of preeminence and one of virtual equality with the other ministers. It is not necessarily true, however, that executive power in presidential systems has to be concentrated in one person, and that the cabinet has to consist of the president's appointees and subordinates. For instance, if the Swiss Federal Council were elected by the voters instead of by parliament, it would be a seven-member presidential executive. Such a collegial presidency, consisting of nine members, was instituted in Uruguay in 1952 and operated until 1967. An example at the subnational level can be found in California, which has a basically presidential form of government—like all of the other American states—and in which not only the governor but several other executive officers, such as the attorney general and the superintendent of public instruction, who are in charge of the departments of justice and education, are popularly elected.

STRENGTHS AND WEAKNESSES OF PARLIAMENTARISM AND PRESIDENTIALISM

The scholarly discussion of the relative strengths and weaknesses of parliamentary and presidential governments has concentrated on two points: the problem of executive instability in parliamentary systems and the problem of executive-legislative deadlock in presidential systems. These problems are inherent, at least potentially, in the two systems and cannot be entirely eliminated, but several measures to alleviate them have been instituted or proposed in a few countries.

1. Because the president in a presidential system is elected for a fixed term of office, a high degree of executive stability is guaranteed. Prime ministers and cabinets in parliamentary systems may also be very stable, as in Great Britain, but in multiparty parliaments without a firm majority coalition, cabinets are

likely to be frequently overthrown. Cabinet instability was endemic in the French Third and Fourth Republics and in the German Weimar Republic. It is not surprising, therefore, that the two regimes that succeeded these republics, the Fifth Republic in France and the West German Federal Republic, included measures to strengthen the cabinet vis-à-vis parliament in their new constitutions.

In the Weimar Republic, cabinets were often brought down by negative majorities: majorities of the right and the left that combined forces against the political center but that were too far apart in their policy preferences to be able to form an alternative coalition cabinet. In order to counteract this source of cabinet instability, the new West German constitution adopted in 1949 prescribes that votes of no confidence must be "constructive." This means that a chancellor can only be dismissed by parliament if a new chancellor is elected simultaneously: "The Bundestag can express its lack of confidence in the Federal Chancellor only by electing a successor with the majority of its members and by requesting the Federal President to dismiss the Federal Chancellor. The Federal President must comply with the request and appoint the person elected."[4] A similar requirement for a constructive vote of no confidence is included in the new democratic constitution of Spain, adopted in 1978.

The parliaments of the French Fourth Republic frequently impeded the cabinet's work by voting against the cabinet's legislative proposals without actually forcing the cabinet to resign—which required an absolute majority vote against the cabinet. The framers of the Fifth Republic constitution eliminated the possibility of such obstruction by giving the cabinet the right to make its proposals matters of confidence, and by stipulating that such proposals be automatically adopted unless an absolute majority of the National Assembly votes to dismiss the cabinet: the government bill "shall be considered as adopted, unless a mo-

4. Article 67, paragraph 1.

tion of censure, filed in the succeeding twenty-four hours, is voted under conditions laid down in the previous paragraph." This previous paragraph prescribes that "the only votes counted shall be those favorable to the motion of censure, which may be adopted only by a majority of the members comprising the Assembly."[5] This procedure for strengthening the cabinet could have been made foolproof by also requiring that motions of censure be "constructive" along the lines of German constitutional rule.

The cabinets in both the Fifth Republic and in postwar Germany have been much more stable than their predecessors. Although the new constitutional provisions may have made at least a small contribution to this change in executive-legislative relations by creating a more positive climate for strong executive authority, the principal explanation is the development of stable and more purposive parties and party coalitions in both countries.

2. Presidential systems solve the problem of executive stability by making the president independent of the legislature, giving him a fixed term of office, and legitimizing his authority by popular election. At the same time, the respective independence of executive and legislature creates the potential of serious disagreements and deadlock between them, which cannot be resolved by removing the chief executive and appointing a new one more in tune with the preferences of the legislature's majority, as in parliamentary forms of government.

In France, the president can try to break a deadlock with the legislature by dissolving the National Assembly and calling for new elections. Because this power tends to tilt executive-legislative relations rather strongly toward executive dominance, it may be wise to give parliament the right to reciprocate and call for the election of a new president. Such a change in the United States Constitution was proposed in 1980 by Lloyd N. Cutler, counsel to President Jimmy Carter: "The President, Vice

5. Article 49, paragraphs 2 and 3.

President, Senators and Congressmen would all be elected for simultaneous six-year terms." In order to break an impasse, "on one occasion each term, the President could dissolve Congress and call for new congressional elections for the remainder of the term. If he did so, Congress, by majority vote of both Houses within 30 days of the President's action, could call for simultaneous new elections for President and Vice President for the remainder of the term."[6]

The logical next step would be to give Congress the right to initiate this procedure, too. It would equalize executive and legislative power in this respect. Such an innovative proposal for improving the presidential form of government was made in a minority report of a Dutch advisory commission on constitutional reform in 1969: both the chief executive and parliament would be popularly elected for four-year terms, but in the case of a deadlock either would have the right to call for the simultaneous election of a new executive and a new legislature.[7] This form of government would have to be classified as Hybrid II in the typology above, because the chief executive would now be dependent on the legislature's confidence. However, since the legislature is equally dependent on the executive's "confidence," premature elections would probably only occur in extreme circumstances, and the essence of presidentialism would be retained. It should be pointed out, of course, that such proposals do not provide foolproof solutions for executive-legislative deadlocks. As Cutler ruefully observes, if according to his plan new presidential and congressional elections were held in order to break an impasse, "the American public might be perverse enough to reelect all the incumbents to office."[8]

6. Lloyd N. Cutler, "To Form a Government," *Foreign Affairs* 59, no. 1 (Fall 1980):141.

7. Arend Lijphart, "Op weg naar een presidentieel stelsel? Opmerkingen over de adviezen van de Staatscommissie Cals-Donner," *Socialisme en Democratie* 27, no. 3 (March 1970):137–43.

8. Cutler, "To Form a Government," p. 141.

EXECUTIVE DOMINANCE VS.
EXECUTIVE-LEGISLATIVE BALANCE

We now come to the most important question: how does the parliamentary-presidential contrast relate to the difference between executive dominance characteristic of the majoritarian model and executive-legislative independence and balance typical of the consensus model? In principle, three patterns of executive-legislative relations can be distinguished: executive dominance, legislative dominance, and a more or less balanced relationship between the two branches of government.

There is no doubt that constitutional separation of powers tends to give the legislature more strength and independence vis-à-vis the executive than does fusion of powers. In particular, the United States Congress is a strikingly powerful legislative body compared with the parliaments of all of the parliamentary systems discussed in this book. With regard to rule-making—the making of both general laws and more detailed regulations—the executives have become dominant in all democratic regimes, but Jean Blondel suggests that about one-third of rule-making may still be "the prerogative of the U.S. Congress," whereas "not more than perhaps 4 or 5 percent of the rule-making can be ascribed to the British parliament or to most parliaments of Western Europe."[9] A comparison of Canada with the United States shows that the weaker position of the Canadian House of Commons and the much lower degree of independence of the individual legislators in Canada must be attributed mainly to its parliamentary form of government, because the two countries are similar in most other important respects—they are both federal states covering large areas with significant regional variations; they both have two major parties that are loose federations of state and provincial parties; neither has a large working-class party; and

9. Jean Blondel, *An Introduction to Comparative Government* (London: Weidenfeld and Nicholson, 1969), pp. 355–56.

so on.[10] The second most powerful legislature to be found in our twenty-two democratic regimes is probably the Swiss parliament, and Switzerland is also the second clear case of separation of powers.

Although separation of power usually also means balance of power, significant shifts in this balance can occur and, in the historical experience of the United States, have actually occurred. Writing in 1884, Woodrow Wilson decried the "central and predominant power" of Congress, and stated that the American "presidential" system should more realistically be called, as the title of his famous book indicates, *Congressional Government*.[11] On the other hand, more recent critics have charged that, especially under Presidents Lyndon B. Johnson and Richard M. Nixon, an "imperial presidency" has tended to overshadow Congress.

In parliamentary systems, the dominance of the cabinet in Britain may be contrasted with the classic example of legislative supremacy and weak cabinets in the French Third and Fourth Republics. Among contemporary democratic regimes, Italy is another, but much less extreme, example of imbalance in favor of the legislature; but the principal contrast nowadays is between executive dominance and executive-legislative balance. K. C. Wheare argues that, in contrast with the Westminster model's fusion of power and cabinet dominance, the more typical pattern in continental Europe "can be best described not as the separation of powers, not as keeping the government out of the legislature, but as keeping the government at arms length in the legislature." This may be called an informal separation of powers or,

10. Leon D. Epstein, *Political Parties in Western Democracies* (New Brunswick, N.J.: Transaction Books, 1980), pp. 330–32.

11. Woodrow Wilson, *Congressional Government: A Study in American Politics* (New York: Meridian Books, 1956), p. 23. See also Eric C. Bellquist, "Congressionalism and Parliamentarism," in John C. Wahlke and Heinz Eulau, eds., *Legislative Behavior: A Reader in Theory and Research* (Glencoe, Ill.: Free Press, 1959), pp. 40–42.

in Wheare's words, an informal "constitutional dualism accepting the independence of legislature and executive."[12]

A potent explanation of this difference is suggested by studies of the independence shown by individual legislators in voting against their own cabinet in Britain. This kind of independent parliamentary behavior has tended to vary directly with the size of the cabinet's majority in the House of Commons: bare-majority cabinets have generally received solid support from their partisans in parliament, whereas cabinets with ample majorities have frequently found their parliamentary party to be more rebellious.[13] The reason is that rebellion against a bare-majority cabinet is dangerous because it may cause the cabinet's defeat and fall. Analogizing from this tendency in the British House of Commons to the other parliamentary systems, we can expect greater legislative independence when cabinets are oversized rather than minimal winning. Similarly, it seems plausible that coalition cabinets will be weaker, and the parliaments that they face relatively stronger, than one-party cabinets. This explanation is particularly intriguing because it links the question of executive-legislative relations, treated in this chapter, to the variable of the different kinds of cabinets, discussed in the previous one.

In order to test the hypothesis we need a measure of the relative power of the executive and the legislature. A rough indicator—but the best one available—is cabinet durability. It may be illustrated by the contrast, mentioned earlier, between the British pattern of executive-legislative relations and that of the French Third and Fourth Republics. Britain has dominant cabinets which are also very durable; France had cabinets dominated by the legislature which were proverbially short-lived. We shall consider a cabinet to remain the "same" cabinet if its party com-

12. K. C. Wheare, *Legislatures* (New York: Oxford University Press, 1963), p. 97.
13. Edward W. Crowe, "Cross-Voting in the British House of Commons: 1945–1974," *Journal of Politics* 42, no. 2 (May 1980):487–510.

TABLE 5.2. Frequency and Average Durability of Four Types of Cabinets in 20 Democracies, 1945–1980

	Average durability (in months)	Number of cabinets
Minimal winning one-party cabinets	74	27
Minimal winning coalition cabinets	46	56
Minority cabinets	19	67
Oversized cabinets	23	68
All cabinets	34	218

Source: Based on data in Jean-Claude Colliard, Les Régimes parlementaires contemporains (Paris: Presses de la Fondation Nationale des Sciences Politiques, 1978), pp. 311–54; Eric C. Browne and John Dreijmanis, eds., Government Coalitions in Western Democracies (New York: Longman, 1982); and Keesing's Contemporary Archives (London: Keesing's Publications).

position does not change, and, as in the previous chapter, we shall take only actual participants in the cabinet, not support parties, into consideration.[14]

Our hypothesis is a threefold one: (1) minimal winning cabinets, which may be one-party or coalition, have a longer average life than oversized cabinets, which are always coalitions; (2) among minimal winning cabinets, the one-party cabinets last longer on the average than the coalition cabinets; and (3) minority cabinets have an average durability between that of oversized and that of minimal winning cabinets. Table 5.2 is based on 218 cabinets in twenty democracies whose cabinets are dependent on legislative confidence—including, therefore, the French Fifth Republic and the Finnish presidential system—and it shows that the first two parts of the hypothesis are borne out. There is a very large difference between the durability of minimal winning one-party cabinets and oversized cabinets: the average life of the latter is only about one-third that of the former. There is also a clear difference between the longevity of minimal winning one-party cabinets

14. Lawrence C. Dodd, Coalitions in Parliamentary Government (Princeton, N.J.: Princeton University Press, 1976), pp. 121–22.

and that of minimal winning coalition cabinets: more than six years (74 months) compared with less than four years (46 months). However, minority cabinets do not have the hypothesized intermediate life span: their average durability is even shorter than that of oversized cabinets, although the difference is relatively small.

The difference between minimal winning and oversized cabinets with regard to cabinet durability also appears when we look at the relationship between the proportion of time that the twenty regimes were governed by minimal winning coalitions (the adjusted percentages of table 4.2) and the average cabinet life in each of the twenty regimes. The correlation coefficient is a strong .71. Table 5.3 summarizes this pattern and identifies the position of each country. Average cabinet life was trichotomized in such a way that the twenty democracies could be divided in three approximately equal groups. The table, too, shows the strength of the relationship: fifteen of the twenty regimes are on the expected diagonal, and only five are slightly deviant. Democracies with a tendency to minimal winning cabinets also tend to have relatively durable cabinets; conversely, democracies that usually have oversized cabinets tend to have more or less short-lived cabinets.

Finland and the Fifth French Republic were included in the above analysis because they have cabinets dependent on the legislature's confidence, and in spite of the fact that they were classified earlier as presidential systems with powerful popularly elected presidents. They are special cases and deserve closer attention. In the French case, it is clearly wrong to interpret its short cabinet durability (29 months) as a sign of the legislature's strength. The pattern of executive-legislative relations that has developed in France since the establishment of the Fifth Republic in 1958 is one of executive dominance quite similar to that found in Britain. The main reason is that the French presidents and their cabinets have so far always been supported by strong parliamentary majorities. As Anthony King states, French cabi-

TABLE 5.3. Usual Types of Cabinets and Average Cabinet
Durability in 20 Democracies, 1945–1980

	Average cabinet life		
	More than 5 years	2.5 to 5 years	Less than 2.5 years
Minimal winning cabinets (more than 85% of the time)	Australia (102) Austria (100) Canada (104) Ireland (70) New Zealand (64) United Kingdom (81)	Iceland (37) Luxembourg (58)	
Minimal winning cabinets (85% of the time or less)	Sweden (74)	Denmark (34) Germany (47) Japan (58) Norway (55)	Belgium (26)
Oversized cabinets		Netherlands (34)	Finland (13) France IV (9) France V (29) Israel (28) Italy (17)

Note: The average cabinet durability for each country is shown in parentheses (in months).

nets "have been sustained in office by majorities almost as solid
as those that sustain British Governments in office. The French
legislature has, if anything, become even more subordinate to the
executive than the British."[15]

This situation would change drastically if a French president were to lose his parliamentary majority—for instance, if the
parties of the left had won the National Assembly elections in
1978 and had insisted on forming a leftist cabinet, or if the parties of the right had triumphed in the National Assembly elections called by Socialist François Mitterrand immediately after

15. Anthony King, "Modes of Executive-Legislative Relations: Great Britain, France, and West Germany," Legislative Studies Quarterly 1, no. 1 (February
1976):21.

his own victory in the 1981 presidential election. The French political scientist Raymond Aron states: "The President of the Republic is the supreme authority as long as he has a majority in the National Assembly; but he must abandon the reality of power to the prime minister if ever a party other than his own has a majority in the Assembly."[16] In such a case, the French presidential form of government would revert to a basically parliamentary system. The Fifth Republic should therefore be described not as "a *synthesis* of the parliamentary and presidential systems" but as an "*alternation* between presidential and parliament phases."[17]

The Finnish political system comes closer to a truly mixed presidential-parliamentary regime, but it is also subject to potentially drastic changes over time. The president of Finland derives his power partly from constitutional provisions but mainly from the fact that Finnish prime ministers and cabinets have tended to be weak and short-lived, and that Finland's proximity to the Soviet Union has required strong foreign policy leadership. As Gordon Smith argues, "a marked decrease in international tension or an unusual increase in government stability" would diminish the stature of the presidency.[18] The effect of such an unlikely development would be that Finland would shift to a more normal parliamentary form of government.

For all nineteen parliamentary regimes, cabinet durability is a good indicator of executive dominance. It does not work well, however, for the Fifth Republic and for Finland. The average Finnish cabinet life of 13 months seriously understates the power of the executive. The actual pattern of executive-legislative relations is much more balanced and resembles that of countries like

16. Raymond Aron, "Alternation in Government in the Industrialized Countries," *Government and Opposition* 17, no. 1 (Winter 1982):8.
17. Maurice Duverger, "A New Political System Model: Semi-Presidential Government," *European Journal of Political Research* 8, no. 2 (June 1980): 186 (italics in original).
18. Gordon Smith, *Politics in Western Europe: A Comparative Analysis*, 2d ed. (London: Heinemann, 1976), p. 110.

Denmark and the Netherlands. Similarly, the average cabinet durability of 29 months in the Fifth Republic gives a false impression of equilibrium; the executive tends to be as dominant as in Britain. The necessary adjustments will be made when the cabinet durability figures are used again in the final chapter to explore the overall patterns of majoritarianism and consensus.

PRESIDENTIALISM AND POWER-SHARING

One of the conclusions of the previous section was that the clearest example of executive-legislative balance, typical of the consensus model of democracy, is found in the American presidential system. Does this mean that presidentialism is particularly compatible with the consensus model? It certainly is to the extent that it implies a thorough separation of powers, but it has one grave drawback: U.S.-style presidentialism concentrates virtually all executive power in the hands of one person. As a result, it is at variance with the first characteristic of the consensus model: executive power-sharing and grand coalitions.

The presidency would have to be made collegial in order to facilitate the consensual requirement of power-sharing. The Swiss Federal Council approximates the ideal type of a power-sharing collegial presidency, but it does not completely fit the "presidential" type because it is not popularly elected. The purest example of a collegial presidency is the colegiado which operated in Uruguay from 1952 to 1967. It was a popularly elected executive body consisting of nine members representing the two major Uruguayan parties. Both the Swiss and the Uruguayan collegial presidencies may be regarded as optimal combinations of the first two characteristics of consensus democracy: executive power-sharing and separation of executive and legislative power.

ADDENDUM: MONARCHS AND PRESIDENTS

The cases of France and Finland, which were difficult to classify in our typology of parliamentary and presidential regimes, have already alerted us to the importance of the question of how much power is exercised by the head of state in a democracy. This section will take a closer look at the different kinds of heads of state and their relative powers, and it will attempt to explain the differences encountered in our set of twenty-two democracies.

The most striking difference is that half of the democratic regimes are monarchies and the other half are republics. The monarchs are mainly kings or queens—represented by a governor-general in Canada, Australia, and New Zealand—but Japan has an emperor and Luxembourg has a grand duke as head of state. It is rather surprising that as many as half of our democracies are monarchies, a constitutional form that appears to be less democratic than republican government. The explanation is that they are constitutional monarchies in which the power of the monarch is extremely limited. Richard Rose and Dennis Kavanagh present the following conclusion: "Monarchs have remained in power where the reigning family has been willing to withdraw from a politically active role. Reciprocally, monarchies have fallen when the monarch has sought to continue to assert political power."[19]

The advantage that the monarchy is frequently claimed to have for a democratic regime is that it provides a head of state who is an apolitical and impartial symbol of unity. For plural societies this may be an asset of considerable importance, since any elected head of state is necessarily a member of one of the subsocieties. On the other hand, monarchs can also be a divisive force. For instance, King Leopold III's behavior during the Second World War became a major political issue in postwar Belgium. In the referendum on whether the king should be retained, held in 1950, the principal subsocieties bitterly opposed each other: the majority of Flemings and Catholics supported the king, and most Walloons, Socialists, and Liberals wanted him removed. Leopold III won the referendum with an overall majority

19. Richard Rose and Dennis Kavanagh, "The Monarchy in Contemporary Political Culture," *Comparative Politics* 8, no. 4 (July 1976):568.

of 58 percent—not a landslide victory for a king!—but he soon abdicated in favor of his son Baudouin.

In terms of basic democratic principles, another disadvantage is that monarchs are not entirely powerless. In parliamentary governments, they generally retain the right to appoint the prime minister. This is not a significant function when there is a unanimous preference for a prime ministerial candidate, but when there is a sudden death or resignation, or when the parties in a multiparty parliament are unable to reach an agreement, the monarch's influence on the eventual choice of a prime minister may be far from negligible. In order to reduce the monarch's role to a purely ceremonial one, the 1974 constitution of Sweden transferred the function of appointing a prime minister from the monarch to the Speaker (chairman) of the Riksdag, the Swedish unicameral parliament: "When a Prime Minister is to be designated the Speaker shall convene representatives of each party group within the Riksdag for consultation. The Speaker shall confer with the Vice Speakers and shall then submit a proposal to the Riksdag. The Riksdag shall proceed to vote on the proposal, not later than on the fourth day thereafter."[20]

Table 5.4 summarizes my conclusion concerning the power of monarchical heads of state: all eleven monarchs are primarily figureheads rather than significant political actors. It also classifies the eleven republics according to two criteria: the method of electing the presidential head of state and the executive power of the president. In six republics, the president is elected by the voters, either directly, as in France, Austria, Iceland, and Ireland, or via an electoral college, as in Finland and the United States. Of the remaining five presidents, four are elected by parliament: those in Israel, Italy, Switzerland, and also in the French Fourth Republic. A slightly different method is used in Germany, where the president is selected by a special federal convention composed of all members of the Bundestag and an equal number of representatives of the parliaments of the Länder.

20. "Instrument of Government," chap. 6, art. 2.

TABLE 5.4. Political Power of Monarchical and Presidential
Heads of State in 22 Democracies

	Weak executive power		Strong executive power
Monarch	Australia Belgium Canada Denmark Japan Luxembourg	Netherlands New Zealand Norway Sweden United Kingdom	
President elected by parliament (or special convention)	France IV Germany Israel Italy		Switzerland
President elected by the voters (or electoral college)	Austria Iceland Ireland		Finland France V United States

Only four of these presidents are powerful executives, and
one of the four, the president of Switzerland, presents a doubtful
case. The Swiss president is elected annually by parliament from
among the members of the Federal Council; traditionally, the seven
councillors serve for one year each on a rotating basis. Election
to the presidency does not add much to a councillor's political
power and influence, but Switzerland still has to be classified
among the countries with a strong and active president since the
president is simultaneously a member of the Federal Council.
However, his power derives entirely from his council membership and not from his presidential office.

With the exception of the Swiss president, the only other
presidential heads of state with important executive powers are
those that are elected by the voters instead of by parliament. Popular election confers democratic legitimacy on a president, and
hence the possibility of assisting the authority granted by the
constitution or even exceeding the constitutional limits. How-

ever, popular election appears to be a necessary but not sufficient condition for a powerful presidency. The directly elected Austrian, Icelandic, and Irish presidents may not be mere figureheads, but their power is relatively weak and limited. In addition to popular election, constitutional and traditional sources of authority and/or a favorable constellation of partisan forces are also required for the creation of a powerful presidency.

We can now relate this discussion of the different types of heads of state to our earlier typology of parliamentary and presidential governments. We found that it was difficult to classify France and Finland, because they appeared to be both parliamentary systems with a prime minister dependent on the legislature's confidence and presidential systems with a popularly elected president. Austria, Iceland, and Ireland—as well as the German Weimar Republic from 1919 to 1933 and contemporary Portugal—also fit this description. Maurice Duverger argues that all these systems should be labeled "semi-presidential governments."[21] It is doubtful that the creation of this special category is really necessary. Especially when the presidents are weak in spite of their popular election—as in Austria, Iceland, and Ireland—the governments operate largely according to the parliamentary model. But Duverger's argument does highlight the potential problem that popularly elected heads of state present for parliamentary governments: popular election may provide the head of state with a democratically legitimate justification to encroach upon or take over leadership of the government, thereby fundamentally changing the nature of the parliamentary regime.

---

21. Duverger, "A New Political System Model: Semi-Presidential Government," pp. 165–87.

6 Parliaments: Concentration vs. Sharing of Legislative Power

The third difference between the Westminster and consensus models of democracy concerns the distribution of power in the legislature. The pure majoritarian model calls for the concentration of legislative power in a single chamber; the pure consensus model is characterized by a bicameral legislature in which power is divided equally between two differently constituted chambers. In practice, we find a variety of intermediate arrangements. Chapters 1 and 2 showed that the New Zealand and Swiss parliaments are, in this respect, perfect examples of majoritarian and consensus democracy respectively, but that our other two main examples deviate from the pure models to some extent. The British parliament is bicameral; but because the House of Lords has little power, it can be described as asymmetrically bicameral. The current Belgian parliament is characterized by a balance of power between the two chambers, but these chambers hardly differ from each other in composition.

The first topics of this chapter will be the simple dichotomous classification of parliaments as bicameral or unicameral as well as several explanations for bicameralism and unicameralism. Next, the differences between the two chambers of bicameral legislatures will be discussed and a more refined classification of parliaments will be proposed. Finally, the relationship between strong bicameralism—that is, bicameralism which is reasonably close to the consensual ideal—and separation of powers, as well as the relationship between strong bicameralism and federalism, will be explored.

One additional introductory comment is in order. Legislative chambers have a variety of proper names (such as House of Commons, House of Representatives, Chamber of Deputies, *Bundestag*, Senate, etc.), and in order to avoid confusion the following generic terms will be used in the discussion of bicameral parliaments: first chamber (or lower house) and second chamber (or upper house). The first chamber is always the more important one or, in federal systems, the house that is elected on the basis of population.[1]

BICAMERAL VS. UNICAMERAL LEGISLATURES

A dichotomous classification of parliaments as bicameral or unicameral appears to be simple and straightforward, but as table 6.1 shows, two countries do not fit either category and, at least provisionally, a third intermediate class must be added. The Norwegian and Icelandic legislatures are elected as one body, but after the election they divide themselves into two "chambers": the Norwegian legislators choose one-fourth, and the Icelandic legislators one-third, of their members to form a "second chamber." It is incorrect, however, to view these two divisions as truly separate chambers of a bicameral parliament. In Norway, for instance, the two divisions have joint legislative committees, and in both countries any disagreements are resolved by a plenary session of all members of the legislature. The upper division is

1. The only potential difficulty of this terminology is that the first chamber of the Dutch parliament is formally called the Second Chamber, and the second chamber is called the First Chamber. Similarly, the first and second chambers of the pre-1970 bicameral legislature of Sweden were called the Second and First Chamber, respectively.

TABLE 6.1. Unicameral, Bicameral, and Hybrid Parliaments in 22 Democracies

Unicameral parliaments	Hybrid parliaments	Bicameral parliaments
Denmark	Iceland	Australia
Finland	Norway	Austria
Israel		Belgium
Luxembourg		Canada
New Zealand		France IV
Sweden		France V
		Germany
		Ireland
		Italy
		Japan
		Netherlands
		Switzerland
		United Kingdom
		United States

therefore not so much a distinct chamber as a "glorified committee" of a "modified unicameral parliament."[2]

Even if we classify the Norwegian and Icelandic legislatures as unicameral—as we shall henceforth do—table 6.1 shows that a majority of the parliaments in our twenty-two democracies are bicameral. On the other hand, there appears to be a trend toward unicameralism. Since the Second World War, three of our countries have shifted from bicameral to unicameral legislatures: New Zealand in 1950, Denmark in 1953, and Sweden in 1970.

What accounts for the adoption and retention of a unicameral instead of a bicameral parliament and vice versa? Since unicameralism is associated with the majoritarian model and bicameralism with the consensus model, we might expect to find bicameralism in plural societies and unicameralism in more homogeneous societies. Table 6.2 shows, however, that there is only

2. These descriptions are borrowed from Gordon Smith, *Politics in Western Europe: A Comparative Analysis*, 2d ed. (London: Heinemann, 1976), p. 167, and Arthur S. Banks and William Overstreet, *Political Handbook of the World: 1980* (New York: McGraw-Hill, 1980), p. 347.

TABLE 6.2. Unicameralism vs. Bicameralism and Extent of
Pluralism in 22 Democracies

	Nonplural society	Semiplural society	Plural society
Unicameral	Denmark Iceland New Zealand Norway Sweden	Finland	Israel Luxembourg
Bicameral	Australia Ireland Japan United Kingdom	Canada France IV France V Germany Italy United States	Austria Belgium Netherlands Switzerland

a weak connection between these variables. Unicameralism does occur more often in nonplural than in plural and semiplural societies, but bicameralism is found with about the same frequency in all three types of society.

Two other explanations of bicameralism are frequently mentioned: the size of a country's population and federalism.[3] The rationale is that second chambers are required to represent the great diversity of interests found in large countries and the interests of the constituent units (states, provinces, cantons, etc.) in federal systems. Table 6.3 relates these two factors to the number of legislative chambers. The classification of the twenty-two democracies into the two approximately equal groups of eleven large and eleven small countries is based on the size of the population: the countries with a population of at least 10 million people are regarded as large.

Both size and federalism are clearly related to bicameralism. All of the large countries and all of the federal systems have

3. See Jean Blondel, Comparative Legislatures (Englewood Cliffs, N.J.: Prentice-Hall, 1973), pp. 32–35; and Gerhard Loewenberg and Samuel C. Patterson, Comparing Legislatures (Boston: Little, Brown, 1979), pp. 120–25.

TABLE 6.3. Unicameralism vs. Bicameralism, Population Size, and Unitary vs. Federal Government in 22 Democracies

	Small countries		Large countries	
	Unitary	Federal	Unitary	Federal
Unicameral	Denmark Finland Iceland Israel Luxembourg New Zealand Norway Sweden			
Bicameral	Ireland	Austria Switzerland	Belgium France IV France V Italy Japan Netherlands United Kingdom	Australia Canada Germany United States

bicameral parliaments. Of the countries that are both small and unitary, almost all are characterized by unicameralism; the only exception is Ireland. When we compare the explanatory power of size and federalism separately, size is the stronger factor. There are only three countries that do not fit the large-bicameral and small-unicameral relationships: Austria, Switzerland, and Ireland are small but they nevertheless have bicameral legislatures. But there are eight cases that deviate from the federal-bicameral and unitary-unicameral links. Belgium, the two French Republics, Italy, Japan, the Netherlands, the United Kingdom, and Ireland are all unitary states, but they have bicameral parliaments.[4]

4. The size of the first or only legislative chamber is also significantly related to population size. The ten larger countries have first chambers with an average membership of 397, whereas the eleven smaller democracies have first or only chambers with an average membership of 158. A slightly different categorization makes this relationship even clearer. The six largest countries, with

VARIETIES OF BICAMERALISM

The two chambers of bicameral legislatures tend to differ in several ways. Originally, the most important function of second chambers, or "upper" houses, elected on the basis of a limited franchise, was to serve as a conservative brake on the more democratically elected "lower" houses; this function has become obsolete in our set of fully democratic regimes, of course. Of the remaining six differences between first and second chambers, three are especially important in the sense that they determine whether or not bicameralism is a significant institution. Let us first take a brief look at the three less important differences:

1. In all but one of the fourteen bicameral legislatures, the second chamber is considerably smaller than the first. The only exception is the British House of Lords, which has more than a thousand members. However, when we exclude the hereditary peers who rarely attend, the number is reduced to approximately 250. Using the latter figure for Britain, the average size of the fourteen second chambers is 155, compared with an average first-chamber membership of 365—almost two and a half times as large.

2. Legislative terms of office tend to be longer in second than in first chambers. The first chamber terms range from two to five years compared with a second chamber range of four to nine years (and, in Britain and Canada, respectively, life membership

populations exceeding 50 million, have first chambers ranging from 435 to 635 members; in this group, the U.S. House of Representatives is the smallest first chamber, although the United States is by far the largest country. The next country, in order of decreasing size, is Canada; its House of Commons has 282 members. The next eleven countries have first or only chambers ranging from 120 to 212 members, with the exception of Sweden, which has an unusually large unicameral legislature of 349 members. The three smallest countries (New Zealand, Luxembourg, and Iceland) have fewer than 100 members in their unicameral legislatures. See George J. Stigler, "The Sizes of Legislatures," *Journal of Legal Studies* 5, no. 1 (January 1976):17–34; and Robert A. Dahl and Edward R. Tufte, *Size and Democracy* (Stanford, Calif.: Stanford University Press, 1973), pp. 80–84.

and membership until retirement). Switzerland is the only, relatively minor, exception: a few of its second-chamber members are elected for terms that are shorter than the four-year term of the first chamber. In all the other bicameral legislatures, the members of second chambers have terms of office that are either longer than or equal to those of the first-chamber members.[5]

3. Another common feature of second chambers is their staggered election. One-half of the membership of the Australian, Dutch, and Japanese second chambers is renewed every three years; the same rule applied in the French Fourth Republic. One-third of the American and French Fifth Republic second chambers is renewed every second and every third year, respectively. Similarly, the members of the Austrian, German, and Swiss federal chambers are selected in a staggered manner but at irregular intervals.

These three differences do affect the way the two chambers of the several legislatures operate. In particular, the smaller second chambers can conduct their business in a more informal and relaxed manner than the usually much larger first chambers. But they do not affect the question of whether a country's bicameralism is a truly strong and meaningful institution. The following three factors do make a major difference in this respect.

1. With regard to their formal powers, second chambers tend to be subordinate to first chambers. For instance, their negative votes on proposed legislation can frequently be overridden by the first chambers, and in parliamentary systems the cabinet may be responsible exclusively to the first chamber. Only four of the thirteen bicameral legislatures have chambers with formally equal

5. The U.S. House of Representatives is exceptional in that it has a short term of office of only two years. Three first or only chambers have three-year terms: in Australia, New Zealand, and Sweden. In the other countries, the members of these chambers may serve as long as four or five years, but in most parliamentary systems premature dissolutions may shorten these maximum terms. The average maximum legislative term of office in the first or only chambers of our twenty-two parliaments is 4.1 years. The average actual term during the 1945–80 period was 3.3 years.

powers: the parliaments of Belgium and Switzerland (the two illustrative cases used in Chapter 2) as well as the Italian and United States legislatures.

2. The actual political importance of second chambers depends not only on their formal constitutional powers but also on their method of selection. All first chambers are directly elected by the voters, but the members of several second chambers are elected indirectly (usually by legislatures at levels below that of the national government) or appointed (like Canadian senators, some of the Irish senators, and life peers in the British House of Lords). Second chambers that are not directly elected lack the democratic legitimacy, and hence the real political influence, that popular election confers. Conversely, the direct election of a second chamber may compensate to some extent for its limited power.

We can construct a threefold classification of bicameral parliaments based on the relative formal powers of the two chambers and the democratic legitimacy of the second chambers. The only fully symmetrical bicameral legislatures are the four, noted above, which have chambers with formally equal powers. Two of these four legislatures also have directly elected second chambers—Italy and the United States—and the majority of the members of the other two second chambers are popularly elected—Belgium and Switzerland. Four bicameral legislatures can be regarded as moderately asymmetrical: those of Australia, Germany, Japan, and the Netherlands. The Australian and Japanese parliaments are elected directly. The Dutch parliament belongs in this category in spite of the second chamber's indirect election by the provincial legislatures, because this chamber has an absolute veto power over all proposed legislation that cannot be overridden by the first chamber. The German second chamber does not owe its strength to either popular election or an absolute legislative veto but to the fact that it is a unique federal chamber, composed of representatives of the *executives* of the member states (*Länder*) of the federation—usually ministers in the member state cabinets. It can thus be described as "one of the most powerful upper chambers in the world."[6] The power relationship between the two houses in the remaining six bicameral parliaments is extremely asymmetrical.

3. The final difference between the two chambers of bicameral legislatures is that second chambers may be designed in such a way as to overrepresent certain minorities. As we shall see in greater detail in chapter 10, second chambers that are federal chambers tend to overrepresent the smaller component units of the federation: the only exception is Austria. Two other second chambers provide special representation for minorities. The overrepresented minority in the British House of Lords is, of course, the nobility; hence the House of Lords has a permanent Conservative majority. The French Senate (like its predecessor in the Fourth Republic) is elected by an electoral college in which the small communes, with less than a third of the total population, have more than half of the votes; on account of this rural overrepresentation, Maurice Duverger has characterized the Senate as the "Chamber of Agriculture."[7] The remaining six countries have chambers that hardly differ from each other in composition. Their bicameralism may be called *congruent*. With only slight variations, both chambers are elected by proportional or semiproportional methods, which are generally favorable to the representation of minorites but do not provide overrepresentation of particular minority groups. Ireland's Senate appears to be an exception, since a large number of senators have to be elected from candidates nominated by vocational and cultural interest groups, but in the electoral college, composed of national and local legislators, party politics predominates. Hence, the Irish Senate "is composed largely of party politicians not very different from their colleagues in the [first chamber] and, in the case

6. Lewis J. Edinger, *Politics in Germany: Attitudes and Processes* (Boston: Little, Brown, 1968), p. 202.

7. Cited in John S. Ambler, *The Government and Politics of France* (Boston: Houghton Mifflin, 1971), p. 165.

TABLE 6.4. Three Types of Bicameralism, Based on the
Congruence and Symmetry of the Two Chambers,
in 14 Democracies

	Incongruent	Congruent
Symmetrical and moderately asymmetrical	Strong bicameralism: Australia Germany Switzerland United States	Weak bicameralism: Belgium Italy Japan Netherlands
Extremely asymmetrical	Weak bicameralism: Canada France IV France V United Kingdom	Insignificant bicameralism: Austria Ireland

of many of them, with only tenuous connections with the interests they affect to represent."[8]

STRONG VS. WEAK BICAMERALISM

The above analysis leads to a distinction between bicameralism
that is strong and significant and weak bicameralism. Strong bicameralism depends on two conditions: the chambers have to be
incongruent in their composition, and they must be symmetrical
or only moderately asymmetrical with regard to their respective
legislative powers. Table 6.4 shows that strong bicameralism can
be found in only four of our countries. Eight bicameral legislatures fail one of the tests: they are either congruent or extremely
asymmetrical, and hence their bicameralism must be regarded as
weak. Two countries have bicameral parliaments that are both
congruent and extremely asymmetrical. This type of bicameral-

8. Basil Chubb, *The Government and Politics of Ireland* (Stanford, Calif.:
Stanford University Press, 1971), p. 205.

ism is completely insignificant and hardly differs from unicameralism.

We now have a threefold typology of parliaments, based on the degree of concentration or sharing of legislative power, that is much more meaningful than the original bicameralism-unicameralism contrast: (1) strongly bicameral legislature, exemplified by four of our twenty-two democracies: Australia, Germany, Switzerland, and the United States; (2) weakly bicameral parliaments, found in eight cases: Belgium, Italy, Japan, the Netherlands, Canada, the two French Republics, and the United Kingdom; and (3) parliaments whose bicameralism is insignificant, as in Austria and Ireland, or that are unicameral, as in the remaining eight countries.

We saw earlier that there is only a weak relationship between the degree of pluralism and the occurrence of bicameralism and unicameralism (see table 6.2). Similarly, the new threefold distinction between parliaments cannot be well explained by whether a society is plural, semiplural, or nonplural. For instance, although strong bicameralism is a characteristic of the consensus model of democracy and is therefore especially suitable for plural societies, only one of our six plural societies (Switzerland) has strong bicameralism, two (Belgium and the Netherlands) have weakly bicameral parliaments, and three (Austria, Israel, and Luxembourg) have unicameral or near-unicameral legislatures.

Population size was found to be a strong explanation of the incidence of bicameralism or unicameralism: all of the eleven larger but only three of the eleven smaller countries have bicameral legislatures (see table 6.3 above). Of the three exceptions—Austria, Ireland, and Switzerland—the first two were classified as having insignificant bicameralism in table 6.4; if these are grouped with the unicameral parliaments, the connection between a small population and unicameralism or insignificant bicameralism, and the connection between large population size and strong or weak bicameralism are even clearer. Switzerland, a small country with strong bicameralism, is now the only deviant case. On the other hand, size does not provide a good explanation for the difference between strong and weak bicameralism. Of the twelve cases with these two types of bicameral parliaments, the seven larger and the five smaller ones each include two cases of strong bicameralism. And both the largest and the smallest in this set of countries—the United States and Switzerland—have strongly bicameral legislatures.

Are there any factors that can give a better explanation for the differential occurrence of strong and weak bicameralism? A closer look at table 6.4 suggests two possible relationships: it is striking that the four cases of strong bicameralism are all federal systems, and that two of the four, Switzerland and the United States, are the two unambiguous examples of separation of powers (see chapter 5). Are these links merely empirical coincidences or can they be logically explained? These questions will be explored in the final two sections of this chapter.

STRONG BICAMERALISM AND SEPARATION OF POWERS

It is often said that there is a fundamental incompatibility between strong bicameralism and the parliamentary form of government. Parliamentarism means that the executive is responsible to parliament and, if it is combined with strong bicameralism, it means that both chambers may claim the power to hold the cabinet responsible. Since strong bicameralism entails two differently constituted chambers, these chambers may have different political majorities, and the cabinet may therefore face the problem of retaining the confidence of two majorities which may disagree with each other. In his classic study of *Legislatures*, K. C. Wheare argues that bicameralism presents no problems if the two chambers are "really chosen on identical lines." Otherwise, he states, parliamentarism "encourages, if indeed it does not require, the supremacy or at least the superiority of one chamber over the other. A cabinet it would seem must be responsible to one chamber: it cannot be responsible to two."[9] In other words, the parliamentary form of government requires that bicameralism be congruent or asymmetrical or both—or, of course, that the legislature be unicameral.

This line of reasoning suggests that the two parliamentary systems classified as strongly bicameral in table 6.4—Australia and West Germany—should be prone to conflict between the institutions of parliamentarism and bicameralism. This tendency appears to be borne out by the Australian constitutional crisis of 1975. In the last months of that year, Prime Minister Gough Whitlam and his Labor party cabinet continued to have the solid backing of their party's majority in the Australian first chamber, the House of Representatives, but the Liberal and Country party coalition had enough votes in the Senate, also a popularly elected chamber, to refuse to pass the government's appropriations bills— and they used this power, for the first time in Australian political history, in an attempt to force Whitlam to resign or to call a new House election which they expected to win. Whitlam and the Labor party took the view that parliamentarism entailed cabinet responsibility to the first chamber only, and hence they steadfastly resisted what they regarded as an illegitimate attempt by the Senate to force them out of office. The governor-general, Sir John Kerr, broke the protracted deadlock by dismissing Whitlam, appointing Liberal leader Malcolm Fraser as a caretaker prime minister, and arranging for new elections of both the House and the Senate. These elections were won decisively by Fraser and his Liberal-Country party coalition.

According to Whitlam and the Labor party, strong bicameralism and parliamentary government could not be reconciled and the principle of parliamentarism should have taken precedence. In contrast to this view, Sir John Kerr saw no basic incompatibility and argued that parliamentarism could mean cabinet respon-

9. K. C. Wheare, *Legislatures* (New York: Oxford University Press, 1963), pp. 201–03.

sibility to both houses of a bicameral parliament. He defended his controversial decision to remove a prime minister who still enjoyed the confidence of the first chamber in the following words: the Senate "undoubtedly has constitutional power to refuse or defer supply to the government, [and] a prime minister who cannot obtain supply . . . must either advise a general election or resign. If he refuses to do this I have the authority and indeed the duty under the Constitution to withdraw his commission as prime minister."[10] But who would have been appointed as prime minister if the December 1975 elections had yielded a House with a Liberal-Country majority and a Senate with a Labor majority, or the other way around? This could have happened, because the two chambers are elected by very different methods: the House is chosen by a majority system in single-member districts, and the Senate by proportional representation in multimember districts (see chapter 9).

Such a situation is also possible, but much less likely, in West Germany. For one thing, the constitution states explicitly that the Bundestag (first chamber) has the power to elect and to dismiss the chancellor. Moreover, the Bundesrat (second chamber) has an absolute veto over only about half of the bills, mainly those affecting the interests of the Länder. With regard to all other legislation, the Bundesrat veto can be overridden by the Bundestag: a veto supported by at least half of the votes in the Bundesrat can be overridden by a normal majority in the Bundestag, and a two-thirds veto by a two-thirds majority to override. This does mean, however, that a basic conflict could arise when the opposition in the Bundestag has more than a third of the seats in this chamber but a two-thirds majority in the Bundesrat: its veto power would then become absolute.

The conclusion therefore seems inescapable that, in the words of one of Australia's most respected political scientists, "govern-

10. Cited in Leon D. Epstein, "The Australian Political System," in Howard R. Penniman, ed., *Australia at the Polls: The National Elections of 1975* (Washington, D.C.: American Enterprise Institute, 1977), p. 45.

ment cannot, in consistency, be simultaneously responsible to two houses elected on different bases at different times, because this can imply (fairly often under the present mode of electing the Senate) responsibility to two mutually hostile majorities."[11] But one crucially important qualification must be added: parliamentarism and strong bicameralism are incompatible only if cabinets tend to be formed on the basis of narrow majorities in the first chamber. If cabinets are grand coalitions, they will have no problem in maintaining the overwhelming support of two quite differently constituted chambers. And oversized cabinets should be able to receive at least majority backing in chambers with contrasting party compositions. In fact, the obvious solution to the problem of "two mutually hostile majorities" in a strong bicameral legislature is to form an oversized coalition cabinet.

In other words, the unqualified assertion that strong bicameralism is incompatible with parliamentarism reveals a majoritarian bias. The conflict is between strong bicameralism and the Westminster form of parliamentarism which prescribes minimal winning cabinets, not between strong bicameralism and the general principle of parliamentary government.

STRONG BICAMERALISM, PARLIAMENTARISM, AND FEDERALISM

Table 6.4 above showed a clear connection between strong bicameralism and federalism: all four countries with strong bicameralism are federal systems, and of the six federations in our set of twenty-two democracies four have strongly bicameral legislatures. The explanation for this link is that one of the characteristics of federalism is a second chamber which serves as a safeguard for the interests of the member states of the federation (see chapter 10). Strong federalism spells a strong federal chamber and hence strong bicameralism.

11. Robert S. Parker, "Political Projections and Partisan Perspectives," *Politics* 11, no. 1 (May 1976):15.

The majoritarian fallacy signaled above can be detected again in the argument that parliamentarism and federalism are incompatible. If federalism entails strong bicameralism, as it ideally does, and if strong bicameralism conflicts with parliamentarism, there does indeed appear to be a contradiction between parliamentary and federal institutions. The logic of this syllogism leads Wheare to an affirmative answer to the following question: "Must it be concluded, then, that in a federation, if it is desired to safeguard states' rights effectively by a second chamber, one must not adopt the cabinet system?"[12] This question actually deserves a qualified negative answer. In principle, there is no contradiction between federalism, strong bicameralism, and the kind of parliamentary government that is characterized by larger than minimal winning cabinets. All three of these institutions are perfectly compatible with each other and with the consensus model.

12. Wheare, *Legislatures*, p. 205.

7 Party Systems: Two-Party and Multiparty Patterns

The fourth and fifth differences between the majoritarian and consensus models of democracy concern related properties of the party systems: the numbers of political parties operating in the system and the differences between them. The majoritarian model is characterized by a two-party system in which the two large parties differ mainly on socioeconomic issues. The consensus model accommodates a larger number of significant parties and a larger number of issues differentiating them, such as religious and cultural issues in addition to socioeconomic ones. The four examples used in chapters 1 and 2—Great Britain, New Zealand, Belgium, and Switzerland—represent close approximations of the pure models, although we shall have to add a few qualifying nuances later in this chapter and in chapter 8. We shall also find many of our twenty-two democratic regimes in intermediate positions between the two pure models.

This chapter will deal with the numbers of parties and their relative sizes. It will first review the reasons why two-party systems are frequently praised in the political science literature and will present a critique of these arguments. Next, it will try to solve the difficult question of which parties should be counted and how they should be counted in order to determine whether a particular country has a two-party system, a three-party system, or a four-party system, and so on. The final topic of the chapter will be the relationships between types of party systems and the first two dimensions differentiating the majoritarian and consensus models, discussed in chapters 4 and 5: the types of

FIGURE 7.1. Majoritarian Propositions concerning the Electoral and Party Systems and Democratic Stability and Quality

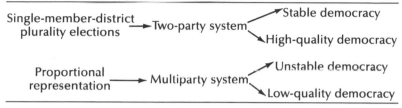

executive coalitions or noncoalitions and of executive-legislative relations.

THE CASE FOR TWO-PARTY SYSTEMS

The traditional literature on party systems is staunchly majoritarian and emphatically favors the two-party system. Its main model is that of the British system, but some of its arguments are also based on the American example. This traditional view is reinforced by a spate of modern comparative studies showing that political regimes with relatively many political parties do not work as well as those with fewer parties. The main arguments are that two-party systems are not only more stable and effective than multiparty systems, but also qualitatively superior in terms of basic democratic values. These propositions are linked further with the type of electoral system, as shown in figure 7.1. Majoritarians prefer the single-member district plurality system, since it favors the two-party system, to proportional representation, which is usually associated with multipartism. Chapter 9 will analyze the relationship between electoral methods and party systems. Here we shall first discuss the alleged virtues of two-party systems with regard to democratic stability and quality:

1. The first advantage of a two-party system is said to be its moderating and centralizing influence on the democratic regime. If there are only two parties competing for the voter's favor, they will tend to concentrate their attention on the uncommitted vot-

ers in the middle of the left-right political spectrum, those between approximately points A and B in figure 7.2. How these floating voters in the center cast their ballots will determine whether the leftist or rightist party will win the election, because most of the voters on the two ends of the spectrum can be safely counted on to support their respective parties. In order to appeal to the uncommitted voters, both parties have to adopt moderate, centrist programs.

This tendency will be strengthened if large numbers of voters are located in the center, as indicated by the bell-shaped curve. If the voters' opinions are divided, as indicated by the second curve (dotted line), the pull toward the center may be less strong but the logic dictating centrist party programs still holds. Even now, for example, if the leftist party adopts an only slightly left-of-center program, the voters to the left of this program will have little choice but to vote for the party. Both parties may, of course, lose some of their supporters at the ends of the spectrum who will decide to abstain instead of voting for what is, to them, a too moderate program. But a vote gained in the center, taken away from the other party, is still twice as valuable as a vote lost by abstention. Whichever party wins can carry out a program that is widely approved by the voters. Moderate policies can also be expected to aid the long-term effectiveness and stability of the regime.

2. In a parliamentary system, like the British, a two-party system has the advantage that the executive will be stable and effective because it will be a cohesive entity consisting of a single party, the majority party, instead of a coalition of parties with divergent interests, and because it will have the backing of a solid majority in Parliament. A. Lawrence Lowell wrote in 1896 that the legislature must contain "two parties, and two parties only, . . . in order that the parliamentary form of government should permanently produce good results." And he called it an "axiom in politics" that coalition cabinets are short-lived compared with one-party cabinets: "the larger the number of discordant groups that form the majority the harder the task of pleasing

FIGURE 7.2. The Moderating Influence of Two-Party Systems

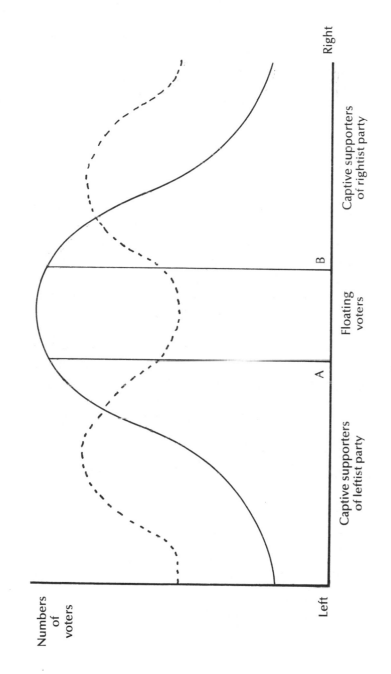

Numbers
of
voters

Captive supporters
of leftist party

A

Floating
voters

B

Captive supporters
of rightist party

Left

Right

them all, and the more feeble and unstable the position of the cabinet."[1] More recent studies have confirmed Lowell's axiom. In fact, we saw earlier that cabinets formed by a majority party—minimal winning one-party cabinets—had a considerably longer life than other types of cabinets during the 1945–80 period (see table 5.3). Several other analyses, using a variety of definitions of cabinet duration and party systems, arrive at the same conclusion: two-party systems are associated with stable cabinets, and as multipartism increases, cabinet life tends to shorten.[2]

3. In a two-party system, the voters can make a clear choice between two alternative sets of public policies. The program of the winning party automatically becomes the government's program. In a multiparty system without a majority party, two or more parties have to negotiate the formation of a majority coalition; the coalition's program will be a compromise between their individual party platforms—a compromise made by political leaders instead of mandated directly by the voters. Two-party systems are therefore more democratic than multiparty systems.

4. A closely related argument in favor of the two-party system is that it makes the majority very powerful but also clearly and unmistakably responsible for the exercise of governmental power. In contrast, accountability for the policies of coalition cabinets in multiparty systems must be shared by all of the parties in the coalition. But they may not be equally responsible, and it may be difficult and confusing for the voters to assign credit or blame to the individual parties. Woodrow Wilson wrote

1. A. Lawrence Lowell, *Governments and Parties in Continental Europe* (Boston: Houghton Mifflin, 1896), 1:70, 73–74.

2. Jean Blondel, "Party Systems and Patterns of Government in Western Democracies," *Canadian Journal of Political Science* 1, no. 2 (June 1968):180–203, esp. 198–200; Michael Taylor and Valentine M. Herman, "Party Systems and Government Stability," *American Political Science Review* 65, no. 1 (March 1971): 28–37; David Sanders and Valentine M. Herman, "The Stability and Survival of Governments in Western Democracies," *Acta Politica* 12, no. 3 (July 1977):346–77; and Lawrence C. Mayer, "Party Systems and Cabinet Stability," in Peter H. Merkl, ed., *Western European Party Systems: Trends and Prospects* (New York: Free Press, 1980), pp. 335–47.

in his classic *Congressional Government*, originally published in 1885: "If there be one principle clearer than another, it is this: that in any business, whether of government or of mere merchandising, *somebody must be trusted*, in order that when things go wrong it may be quite plain who should be punished. . . . *Power and strict accountability for its use* are the essential constituents of good government."[3]

A CRITIQUE OF TWO-PARTY THEORY

The above arguments in favor of two-party systems appear to be strong, but they are weakened by several important counterarguments:

1. One reason why the traditional comparativists in political science believed that successful democracy required a two-party system was their myopic preoccupation with the large democratic countries and with the contrast between the stable British and American two-party systems and the unstable multiparty sytems of the German Weimar Republic, the French Third and Fourth Republics, and postwar Italy. Hence it was tempting to blame the instability of the latter regimes on their multipartism. The more recent inclusion of the smaller democracies in comparative analysis had dispelled this myth. In particular, the Scandinavian and Benelux countries as well as Switzerland have a long history of successful democracy combined with multiparty systems. It is certainly incorrect to view multipartism as a fatal flaw that inevitably undermines democracy.

2. The evidence does show that multipartism is associated with relatively short-lived cabinets, but it is also a mistake to regard such cabinet "instability" as an indicator of fundamental regime instability.[4] This is valid only for the extreme case of cab-

3. Woodrow Wilson, *Congressional Government: A Study in American Politics* (New York: Meridian Books, 1956), pp. 186–87 (italics in original).
4. See Leon Hurwitz, "An Index of Democratic Political Stability: A Methodological Note," *Comparative Political Studies* 4, no. 1 (April 1971):41–68.

inets whose effectiveness is impaired by very frequent turnovers. The French Fourth Republic is the proverbial example: as table 5.3 above shows, its average cabinet life was only nine months. This figure may still be an overstatement, as we used a liberal definition of cabinet durability that considers a cabinet the same if its party composition does not change. Other authors have used one or more of the following three additional criteria to signal the end of a cabinet's life: a change of prime minister, an intervening parliamentary election, and any cabinet resignation. The application of all these reduces the life of Fourth Republic cabinets to an average of seven months.

However, even this extreme case should not be exaggerated. Especially in retrospect, the Fourth Republic and its cabinets were far from completely ineffective. For one thing, many members of each defunct cabinet served again in the new one, and their average life as ministers was considerably longer than that of the cabinets as a whole. The contemporary French observer André Siegfried explained this "paradox of stable policy with unstable cabinets" as follows: "Actually the disadvantages are not as serious as they appear to foreign observers. When there is a cabinet crisis, certain ministers change or the same ministers are merely shifted around; but no civil servant is displaced, and the day-by-day administration continues without interruption. Furthermore, as the same ministers hold over from one cabinet to another, they form as it were teams of government."[5]

Conversely, long-lived cabinets do not necessarily indicate great regime stability either. Another extreme case provides a telling example: the fifty-one-year rule of the Unionists in Northern Ireland from 1921 to 1972 far exceeded the cabinet life of any of the countries in table 5.3. Yet instead of making for a stable democratic regime, the Unionist government was less and less able to cope with Northern Ireland's problems, and ended in a

5. André Siegfried, "Stable Instability in France," Foreign Affairs 34, no. 3 (April 1956):399.

civil war. *If cabinet durability is an indicator of anything, it shows the dominance of the cabinet over the legislature,*as we have discussed it in chapter 5. The majoritarians' confusion of cabinet stability with regime stability may be partly explained in terms of their preference for powerful and dominant executives.

3. With regard to the argument that two-party systems are optimal for democratic quality, it should be pointed out that there is a contradiction between two of the claims of two-party system advocates: the assertion that both parties will be moderate and centrist and the claim that they offer a clear choice between alternative programs. If their programs are both close to the political center, they will be very similar to each other: instead of offering a meaningful "choice" to the voters, the parties in a two-party system may simply "echo" each other. It should be pointed out, of course, that most two-party theorists do not make both of the competing claims simultaneously. The advantage of party moderation is typically asserted by the American school of thought, whereas the claim of a clear-cut choice reflects the British two-party school.

4. Moreover, a two-party system is neither a necessary nor a sufficient condition for clear party responsibility for government actions. A multiparty system may also have a majority party capable of forming a minimal winning one-party cabinet. What is more important is that a two-party system guarantees unambiguous governmental responsibility only under special circumstances—all of which entail majoritarian assumptions. First, the majority party must choose to form a cabinet by itself instead of forming a grand coalition with the minority party. To be sure, this is what majority parties usually do, but there are significant exceptions, such as the British Conservatives and Swedish Socialists during the Second World War and the Austrian Catholic People's party from 1945 to 1949. Second, clear one-party responsibility presupposes a parliamentary system. In a presidential system with a separately elected executive and legislature,

the executive may belong to one party while the other party has a legislative majority. Responsibility for government policy is then necessarily shared. Third, power-sharing and the sharing of responsibility by the two parties may also occur in cases of strong bicameralism with two powerful and differently constituted houses: one party may control the first and the other the second chamber. Fourth, the two parties must be cohesive entities respectively supporting and opposing the government's program. For instance, even when the American presidency, Senate, and House are all "controlled" by the same party, most legislation is passed by shifting bipartisan majorities with bipartisan minorities in the opposition—again precluding the assignment of responsibility to one party. In most respects, therefore, the claim of clear party responsibility can be made only by a two-party theory based on the British instead of on the American model.

5. Finally, the case for two-party systems relies heavily on the majoritarian assumption that there is only one significant issue dimension in the political system, the left–right spectrum. The two parties can then offer moderate leftist and rightist alternatives to the voters. If there are both a left–right dimension and, for instance, a foreign-policy dimension such as proalignment versus proneutralism, and if these dimensions do not coincide, two parties are unable to present all four alternatives to the voters: proalignment left, proneutralist left, proalignment right, and proneutralist right. Such a situation does not worry the two-party theorists of the American school: they want parties to incorporate several issue dimensions in order to moderate policy preferences within the parties. The logic of the British school of thought, which emphasizes the need of clear-cut alternatives for the electorate, can support a two-party system only in a one-dimensional competition between parties. If partisan conflict is multidimensional, a two-party system must be regarded as an electoral straitjacket that can hardly be regarded as democratically superior to a multiparty system reflecting all of the major issue alternatives.

WHICH PARTIES SHOULD BE COUNTED?

So far we have compared the merits of two-party and multiparty systems without drawing a precise dividing line between them. Pure two-party systems with, in Lowell's words quoted above, "two parties, and two parties only," are rare. In practice, party systems like the British, American, and Australian are usually also considered to be two-party systems. There are three problems: (1) Should small parties be counted? (2) Should an uncohesive or faction-ridden party be regarded as a single party? (3) Should two closely and continuously allied parties be counted as one or two parties? The first of these questions is the most important one and will be treated at length in the next section. The other two can be answered more briefly, and will be dealt with first.

Political parties differ a great deal with regard to their internal cohesion. For instance, the disciplined British parties and the fragmented American parties are a world apart. Can we still refer to both as two-party systems? If not, what are the alternatives? It has been suggested that the American party system is more like a four-party system consisting of liberal Democrats, conservative Democrats, liberal Republicans, and conservative Republicans; or a six-party system with left, center, and right wings in each party; or even a hundred-party system with different Democratic and Republican parties in each state. All of these suggestions are rather artificial and do not really clarify the situation. A similar problem occurs when parties are divided into clearly identifiable factions, such as the Italian Christian Democrats and the Japanese Liberal Democrats. Are these factions the real parties? Such a suggestion again represents an extreme view. Since there is no good solution, the best approach is generally to regard as parties those entities that call themselves "parties," but to remember that they may range from highly disciplined and cohesive organizations to very loose alliances.

There is a simple and sensible solution to the problem of

two parties with different party names that tend to work together so closely that they appear to be a single unit. The most important examples are the Liberal and Country parties in Australia and the German Christian Democratic Union and the Christian Social Union; the CSU is the Christian Democratic party in Bavaria. Both of these party combinations have long histories of cooperation in elections, in governments, and in oppositions. The best criterion is to look at their organization in the legislature; if they maintain separate party caucuses in parliament, they must be considered different parties (the case of the Liberal and Country parties); if they join into one parliamentary party group, they must be counted as a single party (the usual situation in the CDU-CSU).[6] In this book, therefore, the CDU-CSU will be treated as one party; the Liberal and Country parties, as two.

THE "EFFECTIVE" NUMBER OF PARTIES

The most important problem in determining the number of parties in a party system is whether to count small parties and, if not, how large a party has to be in order to be included in the count. For instance, in the 1979 election of the British House of Commons, ten parties succeeded in getting representation in the House. If we still call the British party system a two-party system, we obviously ignore eight of these ten parties, including the Liberals, who gained 13.8 percent of the vote and eleven seats.

One well-known solution has been proposed by Giovanni Sartori. He suggests, first of all, that parties which fail to win seats in parliament be disregarded, that the relative strengths of the other parties be measured in terms of parliamentary seats, that not all parties regardless of size can be counted, but that one cannot establish an arbitrary cut-off point of say 5 or 10 percent above which parties are counted and below which they should be ignored. These preliminary assumptions are unexceptionable.

6. See Carol Carl-Sime, "Bavaria, the CSU and the West German Party System," *West European Politics* 2, no. 1 (January 1979): 89–107.

More controversial, however, are his "rules for counting." He argues that only those parties should be counted as parts of the party system that have either "coalition potential" or "blackmail potential." A party has coalition potential if it has participated in governing coalitions (or, of course, in one-party governments), or if the major parties regard it as a possible coalition partner. In addition, parties that are ideologically unacceptable to all or most of the other coalition partners, and which therefore lack coalition potential, must still be counted if they are large enough. Examples are the strong French and Italian Communist parties during most of the postwar era. This is Sartori's "subsidiary counting rule based on the power of intimidation, or more exactly, the *blackmail potential* of the opposition-oriented parties."[7]

Sartori's criteria are very useful for distinguishing between the parties that are truly relevant in the political system and those that play only a minor role; the next chapter on the dimensionality of party systems will use them for this purpose. But they are not satisfactory for counting the number of parties in a party system. It should be pointed out first that, although Sartori's criteria are based on two variables, size and ideological compatibility, the size factor is the crucial one. This is shown in table 7.1. Very small parties with only a few seats in the legislature may be quite moderate and hence ideologically acceptable to most other parties, but they rarely possess coalition potential because they simply do not have sufficient "weight" to contribute to a cabinet. Hence the parties to be counted, whether or not they are ideolog-

---

7. Giovanni Sartori, *Parties and Party Systems: A Framework for Analysis* (Cambridge: Cambridge University Press, 1976), 1:122–23 (italics in original). Sartori is too critical of his own criterion of coalition potential when he states that it is merely "postdictive," since "the parties having a coalition potential, coincide, in practice, with the parties that have in fact entered, at some point in time, coalition governments" (p. 123). For example, immediately after the first electoral success of the Dutch party Democrats '66 in 1967, it was widely regarded as an acceptable coalition partner, although it did not actually enter a cabinet until 1973.

TABLE 7.1. Criteria of Coalition and Blackmail Potential

| | | Ideological compatibility | |
		Yes	No
Sufficiently large size	Yes	Coalition potential	Blackmail potential
	No	Neither coalition nor blackmail potential	

ically compatible, are mainly the larger ones. However, although the size factor figures so prominently in Sartori's thinking, he does not use it to make further distinctions among the relevant parties: for instance, both the dominant Christian Democratic party of Italy and its frequent but very small coalition partner, the Republican party, which has never won more than 2.5 percent of the lower house seats since 1948, are counted equally.

In order to remedy this defect, Jean Blondel has proposed a classification of party systems that takes into account both their number and their relative sizes. His four categories are shown in table 7.2. Two-party systems are dominated by two large parties, although there may be some other small parties in parliament. Examples are the United Kingdom, the United States, New Zealand, and Austria. If, in addition to the two large parties, there is a considerably smaller party but one that may have coalition potential and that plays a significant political role—such as the German and Luxembourg Liberals, the Irish Labour party, and the Canadian New Democrats—Blondel calls this a "two-and-a-half" party system. Another example of a "half" party is the Australian Country party, although Blondel himself classifies Australia as a two-party system, based on the questionable assumption that the Liberal and Country parties form a single party. As we regard the Country party as a separate party, Australia must be placed in the two-and-a-half party category.

Systems with more than two-and-a-half significant parties are multiparty systems, and these can be subdivided further into multiparty systems with and without a dominant party. Blon-

TABLE 7.2. Classification of Party Systems Based on the
Numbers and Relative Sizes of Political Parties

Party Systems	Hypothetical examples of seat shares	Effective number of parties
Two-party system	55 - 45	2.0
Two-and-a-half party system	45 - 40 - 15	2.6
Multiparty system with a dominant party	45 - 20 - 15 - 10 - 10	3.5
Multiparty system without a dominant party	25 - 25 - 25 - 15 - 10	4.5

Source: Adapted from Jean Blondel, "Party Systems and Patterns of Government in Western Democracies," *Canadian Journal of Political Science* 1, no. 2 (June 1968):184–87.

del's examples of the former are Italy, with its dominant Christian Democratic party; the three Scandinavian countries, with their strong Socialist parties; and Iceland, where the Independents have long been the strongest party among several weaker ones. The French Fifth Republic, Japan since the late 1960s, and Israel until the mid-1970s provide additional examples. Multiparty systems without a dominant party exist in Switzerland, the Netherlands, Finland, and the French Fourth Republic. Blondel classifies Belgium as a two-and-a-half party system, with the Liberals serving as the "half" party. As a result of the fragmentation of the Belgian party system in the 1970s, it must now be regarded as a multiparty system without a dominant party.[8]

The concepts of a "dominant" party and a "half" party are extremely useful in highlighting, respectively, the relatively strong

8. See Blondel, "Party Systems and Patterns of Government," pp. 184–87. It should be noted that Blondel's classes are not logically exhaustive; for instance, there is no category for systems with three equally strong parties or for multiparty systems with two dominant parties. But the four classes do capture most of the empirical cases, with only the Netherlands constituting a partial exception; in a different work, Blondel calls the Dutch party system "transitional" between the third and fourth categories; see his *An Introduction to Comparative Government* (London: Weidenfeld and Nicolson, 1969), p. 157.

and relatively weak position of one of the parties compared with the other important parties in the system, but they are still rather imprecise. What we need is an index that tells us exactly how many parties there are in a party system, taking their relative sizes into account. Fortunately, there is such an index, developed by Markku Laakso and Rein Taagepera, which yields a figure that they call the "effective number of parties." This number equals

$$\frac{1}{\sum\limits_{i=1}^{n} p_i^2}$$

in which p_i is the proportion of seats of the $i-$ th party.[9]

It can be easily seen that in a two-party system with two equally strong parties, the effective number of parties is exactly 2.0. If one party is considerably stronger than the other, with, for instance, respective seat shares of 70 and 30 percent, the effec-

9. Markku Laakso and Rein Taagepera, "'Effective' Number of Parties: A Measure with Application to West Europe," *Comparative Political Studies* 12, no. 1 (April 1979):3–27. The effective number of parties (N) carries the same information as Douglas W. Rae and Michael Taylor's index of fragmentation (F) and can easily be calculated from F as follows:

$$N = \frac{1}{1-F}.$$

The advantage of N is that it can be visualized more easily as the number of parties than the abstract Rae-Taylor index of fragmentation. N is also similar to John K. Wildgen's index of hyperfractionalization (I). N and I yield exactly the same values when all parties are equally strong; in other situations, the values of I tend to be higher than those of N. An advantage of N is that its lower values are more realistic. For instance, a system of three parties with 45, 45, and 10 percent of the seats appears to be closer to a two-party than a three-party system; the N for this case reflects this characteristic rather well by its value of 2.4, whereas the I equals 2.6. Another advantage of N is that it is much easier to calculate. See Douglas W. Rae and Michael Taylor, *The Analysis of Political Cleavages* (New Haven, Conn.: Yale University Press, 1970), pp. 22–44; and John K. Wildgen, "The Measurement of Hyperfractionalization," *Comparative Political Studies* 4, no. 2 (July 1971):233–43.

tive number of parties is 1.7—in accordance with our intuitive judgment that we are moving away from a pure two-party system in the direction of a one-party system. Similarly, with three exactly equal parties, the effective number formula yields a value of 3.0. If one of these parties is weaker than the other two, the effective number of parties will be somewhere between 2.0 and 3.0, depending on the relative strength of the third party. In the hypothetical example of the two-and-a-half party system in table 7.2—with three parties holding 45, 40, and 15 percent of the parliamentary seats—the effective number of parties is in fact very close to two and a half, namely 2.6.

In all cases where all of the parties are exactly equal, the effective number will be the same as the raw numerical count. When the parties are not equal in strength, the effective number will be lower than the actual number. This can also be seen in table 7.2. The two hypothetical examples of multiparty systems contain five parties each. When there is a dominant party, the effective number of parties is only 3.5. Without a dominant party, the seat shares are more equal and the effective number increases to 4.5, close to the raw number of parties in which all parties are counted regardless of size.

Table 7.3 shows the effective number of parties, averaged over all elections between 1945 and 1980, in twenty-two democratic regimes. They are listed in increasing order of effective party numbers. This order corresponds closely with Blondel's four categories: his two-party systems are at the top and his multiparty systems without a dominant party at the bottom of the table. In the middle, only Belgium and Luxembourg are not in the expected order, the latter because its third party has tended to be stronger than the usual "half" party, the former because of its shift from a two-and-a-half party system in the 1950s (exactly 2.5 in 1958) to a multiparty system without a dominant party in the 1970s. In most of the other countries, too, the effective number of parties fluctuated to at least some extent during the 1945–80 period, but no overall trend toward an increase or decrease in

TABLE 7.3. Average, Lowest, and Highest Effective Numbers of Parliamentary Parties resulting from Elections in 22 Democracies, 1945–1980

	Mean	Lowest	Highest
United States	1.9	1.8	2.0
New Zealand	2.0	1.9	2.0
United Kingdom	2.1	2.0	2.3
Austria	2.2	2.1	2.5
Canada	2.4	1.5	2.9
Australia	2.5	2.4	2.7
Germany	2.6	2.2	4.0
Ireland	2.8	2.4	3.6
Japan	3.1	2.0	5.8
Sweden	3.2	2.9	3.5
Norway	3.2	2.7	4.1
Luxembourg	3.3	2.7	4.1
France V	3.3	1.7	4.6
Italy	3.5	2.6	4.4
Iceland	3.5	3.2	3.9
Belgium	3.7	2.5	6.8
Denmark	4.3	3.5	6.9
Israel	4.7	3.4	6.0
France IV	4.9	4.2	5.9
Netherlands	4.9	3.7	6.4
Switzerland	5.0	4.7	5.5
Finland	5.0	4.5	5.6

Source: Based on data in Thomas T. Mackie and Richard Rose, *The International Almanac of Electoral History* (London: Macmillan, 1974); *European Journal of Political Research* 2-9, no. 3 (September 1974–81); and John F. Bibby, Thomas E. Mann, and Norman J. Arnstein, *Vital Statistics on Congress, 1980* (Washington, D.C.: American Enterprise Institute, 1980), pp. 6–7.

the number of parties can be discerned. Of the countries with a wide range of numbers of parties, there was a trend toward consolidation in Germany, Ireland, Israel, and Japan, a trend toward fragmentation in Belgium and Denmark, and strong ups and downs without any clear trend in Canada and the French Fifth Republic.

It should be emphasized that the effective numbers of parties listed in table 7.3 and discussed so far in this chapter refer to the political parties as they are represented in the first or only chambers of the legislatures and are calculated on the basis of their parliamentary seats. It is also possible to calculate the effective number of parties based on their vote shares instead of seat shares. We shall refer to the number based on vote shares as the effective number of *electoral* parties in contrast with the effective number of *parliamentary* parties. Chapter 9 will look into the relationship between the two. Here it should be pointed out that the effective number of electoral parties may fluctuate much more than the number of parliamentary parties. In particular, some of the numbers in table 7.3 that appear very stable do not reflect substantial variations at the electoral level. The highly stable British two-party system, with a narrow range of variation between 2.0 and 2.3 parties, is a case in point. Chapter 1 stressed that the dominance of the two major parties in Britain declined during the 1970s. This trend shows up rather weakly in the average number of parliamentary parties, which was 2.0 in the elections of the 1950s and 1960s and increased to 2.2 in the 1970s. In contrast, the average number of electoral parties was 2.3 in the 1950s and 1960s but 2.9 in the 1970s.

PARTY SYSTEMS AND TYPES OF CABINETS

Our earlier discussion of the case for two-party systems cited evidence linking the number of parties with different types of cabinets and with cabinet longevity. This evidence meshes with the main theme of this book; we would expect the majoritarian characteristic of a two-party system or, more generally, a small effective number of parliamentary parties, to go together with the other majoritarian characteristics of minimal winning cabinets and executive dominance as indicated by long cabinet durability. Conversely, the consensual characteristics of a relatively large number of parliamentary parties should be related to oversized and less durable cabinets. Let us see how strong these relationships are.

Lowell's argument was that multiparty systems without a

majority party necessitate coalition government. In our twenty-one democratic regimes with cabinets selected by the legislature (including all of our cases except the United States) there is indeed a strong relationship between the effective number of parties and the percentage of time during which cabinets were coalitions in the 1945–80 period. The correlation coefficient is .61.

A more interesting potential link is that between the number of parties and not just any coalition government but oversized coalitions. Lowell's theory does not predict such a relationship, as he assumes that, in the absence of a majority party, coalitions are needed to build a *bare* parliamentary majority—completely in line, of course, with the coalition theories discussed in chapter 4. On the other hand, the majoritarian-consensual contrast does lead us to expect this relationship. For the twenty-one democratic regimes, the coefficient of correlation between the effective number of parties and the adjusted percentage of time during which the country was ruled by minimal winning cabinets (see table 4.2) is .84—a much stronger relationship than the .61 between multipartism and any type of coalition.

Table 7.4 shows how each regime fits the pattern; the party systems are trichotomized, using 3.0 and 4.0 parties as the dividing lines. Of the twenty-one democracies, fifteen are located on the expected diagonal, and only six are slightly deviant. The two completely deviant cells are empty. Another way to express this strong relationship is to state that countries with fewer than 3.0 parties are ruled by minimal winning cabinets 89 percent of the time, those with between 3.0 and 4.0 parties 70 percent of the time, and those with more than 4.0 parties only 28 percent of the time.

PARTY SYSTEMS AND CABINET DURABILITY

In the twenty countries for which cabinet durability is a meaningful concept (excluding Switzerland and the United States), there is also a strong relationship between the effective number

TABLE 7.4. Effective Number of Parties and Usual Types of Cabinets in 21 Democracies, 1945–1980

	Fewer than 3.0 parties	3.0 to 4.0 parties	More than 4.0 parties
Minimal winning cabinets (more than 85% of the time)	Australia (2.5) Austria (2.2) Canada (2.4) Ireland (2.8) New Zealand (2.0) United Kingdom (2.1)	Iceland (3.5) Luxembourg (3.3)	
Minimal winning cabinets (85% of the time or less)	Germany (2.6)	Belgium (3.7) Japan (3.1) Norway (3.2) Sweden (3.2)	Denmark (4.3)
Oversized cabinets		France V (3.3) Italy (3.5)	Finland (5.0) France IV (4.9) Israel (4.7) Netherlands (4.9) Switzerland (5.0)

Note: The effective number of parties is shown in parentheses.

of their parties and the durability of their cabinets. The correlation coefficient is −.80; the sign is negative because, as the number of parties increases, cabinet durability—and executive dominance—decrease.

Table 7.5 presents the overall pattern and how each regime fits it. The dividing lines are again at 3.0 and 4.0 parties (as in table 7.4) and at average cabinet durabilities of 2.5 and 5.0 years (as in table 5.3). The cells on the expected diagonal contain thirteen of the twenty cases. Seven countries are slightly off the diagonal, but again there are no completely deviant cases. Democracies with relatively few parties have an average cabinet durability of 81 months, those in the intermediate category 44 months, and those with the largest number of parties only 24 months.

Clearly, the effective number of parties is closely related both

TABLE 7.5. Effective Number of Parties and Average Cabinet
Durability in 20 Democracies, 1945–1980

		Fewer than 3.0 parties	3.0 to 4.0 parties	More than 4.0 parties
Average cabinet life	More than 5.0 years	Australia (2.5) Austria (2.2) Canada (2.4) Ireland (2.8) New Zealand (2.0) United Kingdom (2.1)	Sweden (3.2)	
	2.5 to 5.0 years	Germany (2.6)	Iceland (3.5) Japan (3.1) Luxembourg (3.3) Norway (3.2)	Denmark (4.3) Netherlands (4.9)
	Less than 2.5 years		Belgium (3.7) France V (3.3) Italy (3.5)	Finland (5.0) France IV (4.9) Israel (4.7)

Note: The effective number of parties is shown in parentheses.

to cabinet type and to cabinet durability. The next two chapters
will show that the number of parties is also intimately linked
with two other variables on which the majoritarian and consensus models of democracy differ: the number of issue dimensions
and the electoral system.

Party Systems:
The Issue Dimensions of **8**
Partisan Conflict

In the majoritarian model of democracy, the political parties typically differ from each other along a single issue dimension, the socioeconomic or left–right dimension. In contrast, partisan differences in the consensus model are multidimensional. This chapter will analyze the seven issue dimensions that occur in one or more of our twenty-two democratic regimes, and it will attempt to determine the relative salience of the two most frequent dimensions: the socioeconomic and the religious. We shall find that the socioeconomic dimension tends to predominate but that strictly unidimensional party systems are rare. The final section of the chapter will discuss the relationship between the effective number of parties and the number of issue dimensions in the twenty-two democracies.

SEVEN ISSUE DIMENSIONS

How can the contents and intensity of party programs and the issue dimensions of party systems be identified? Official party platforms or manifestoes should be read with some skepticism, but they do offer some clues to where parties stand on public policies, especially if they are supplemented by other formal party pronouncements, debates in party conferences, and speeches by party leaders in parliament and elsewhere. Moreover, we can observe the actual policies pursued by a party when it is in power or the policies promoted by a party when it shares governmental power with one or more partners in a coalition. Party programs must be distinguished from the characteristics of the voters that parties represent. For instance, the fact that a party receives exceptionally strong support from Roman Catholic voters does not automatically make it a Catholic party or necessarily indicate that religion is an important issue dimension. On the other hand, there is usually a mutual relationship between a party's program and the objective and subjective interests and needs of the party's supporters.

A second guideline for the identification of the issue dimensions of party systems is that we should focus on the differences between rather than within parties. This means that some important sets of issues in a country may not constitute issue dimensions of its party system: they may divide parties internally instead of from each other. Third, we shall restrict our analysis to the political issues dividing the significant or "relevant" parties—parties that have either coalition or "blackmail" potential (see chapter 7). Finally, we shall focus on the durable issue dimensions of party systems and ignore partisan differences that may emerge in one election but fade away soon afterward.

The following issue dimensions were present in at least some of the twenty-two democratic party systems in the 1945–80 period:

1. Socioeconomic
2. Religious
3. Cultural-ethnic
4. Urban-rural
5. Regime support
6. Foreign policy
7. Postmaterialism

The first six of these dimensions correpond closely with the lasting party-system cleavages identified by several other authors.[1] The seventh is the new cleavage between "materialists" and "postmaterialists" which Ronald Inglehart has found to be of great, and probably growing, significance in industrialized societies.

The presence of one or more of these seven issue dimensions in the party systems of our twenty-two democratic regimes is indicated in table 8.1. A distinction is made between dimensions of high salience (H) and those of only medium intensity (M). The judgments on which the table is based are necessarily subjective, but most of them are straightforward and uncontroversial. The few difficult cases will be pointed out in the discussion of each of the issue dimensions below.

THE SOCIOECONOMIC DIMENSION

There are four leftist vs. rightist party positions on socioeconomic policy: (1) governmental vs. private ownership of the means of production; (2) a strong vs. a weak governmental role in economic planning, (3) support of vs. opposition to the redistribution of wealth from the rich to the poor; and (4) the expansion of vs. resistance to governmental social welfare programs.[2] The dimension comprising these four basic components is listed first in table 8.1, because it is the most important of the issue dimensions and because it was present in all of the democratic party systems from 1945 to 1980.

This conclusion appears to contradict the so-called end of

1. Giovanni Sartori, *Parties and Party Systems: A Framework for Analysis* (Cambridge: Cambridge University Press, 1976), 1:336–37; Michael Taylor and Michael Laver, "Government Coalitions in Western Europe," *European Journal of Political Research* 1, no. 3 (September 1973):237–48; Lawrence C. Dodd, *Coalitions in Parliamentary Government* (Princeton, N.J.: Princeton University Press, 1976), p. 99.

2. Robert Harmel and Kenneth Janda, *Comparing Political Parties* (Washington, D.C.: American Political Science Association, 1976), pp. 33–35. The first three components coincide with what Martin Seliger calls the three socioeconomic "core-issues" of the left–right dimension; see Seliger, *Ideology and Politics* (London: Allen and Unwin, 1976), pp. 214–16.

TABLE 8.1. Issue Dimensions of 22 Democratic Party Systems, 1945–1980

	Socio-economic	Religious	Cultural-ethnic	Urban-rural	Regime support	Foreign policy	Post-materialist	Number of dimensions
Australia	H	M		H				2.5
Austria	H	H						2.0
Belgium	H	H	H					3.0
Canada	M		H					1.5
Denmark	H			H		M		2.5
Finland	H		H	H	M			3.5
France IV	H	H		M	H	H		4.5
France V	H	H			M	H		3.5
Germany	H	H						2.0
Iceland	H			H		H		3.0
Ireland	M					M		1.0
Israel	H	H				H		3.0
Italy	H	H			M	M		3.0
Japan	H	M			M	H		3.0
Luxembourg	H	H						2.0
Netherlands	H	H					H	3.0
New Zealand	H							1.0
Norway	H	H		H			M	3.5
Sweden	H			H			M	2.5
Switzerland	H	H	M	M				3.0
United Kingdom	H					M		1.5
United States	M		M					1.0
Total	20.5	12.0	4.0	7.0	3.0	7.0	2.0	55.5

Note: H indicates a dimension of high salience;
M means a medium-salience dimension.

ideology theory, formulated and widely accepted in the 1960s. This theory held that leftist, especially socialist, thinking had been transformed from a true ideology—a consistent, systematic, and comprehensive set of political principles—into a more pragmatic and moderate program, and that the formerly wide gap between socialist and conservative policy preferences had narrowed dramatically. The term "end of ideology" is a hyperbole, of course; it is more accurate to speak of a decline of ideology. Such a decline, fueled by the unprecedented growth in economic prosperity of the industrialized democracies in the 1950s and early 1960s, occurred particularly with regard to the question of government ownership of the means of production. In addition, the leftist positions on economic planning, income redistribution, and social welfare programs—as well as the rightist responses to these policy preferences—have become more moderate. Seymour M. Lipset, writing in 1964, argues that this convergence of socioeconomic ideologies marks the development of the new ideological agreement of "conservative socialism," which he calls "the ideology of the major parties of Europe and America."[3]

With the advantage of hindsight, this judgment—which was partly a description and partly a prediction—appears to have been premature. For one thing, the economic problems of the 1970s and early 1980s have strengthened left–right tensions. Moreover, even though the objective growth of the total economic pie makes its division among different groups and classes in society easier, the economic expectations of these groups remain subjective and relative. As Lipset himself emphasizes, "as long as some men are rewarded more than others by the prestige or status structure of society, men will feel relatively deprived.[4] There has also been a growing awareness that economic prosperity and the distribution of prosperity are to a large extent politically determined, and this has increased the salience of socioeconomic issues as a dimension of partisan conflict.

The importance of political influences on economic policies and performance has been confirmed by several studies of the political-economic nexus. They show significant differences between the socioeconomic policies pursued by leftist-oriented and

3. Seymour Martin Lipset, "The Changing Class Structure and Contemporary European Politics," in Stephen R. Graubard, ed., A New Europe? (Boston: Houghton Mifflin, 1964), p. 362 (italics in original).

4. Seymour Martin Lipset, Political Man: The Social Bases of Politics (Garden City, N.Y.: Anchor Books, 1963), pp. 444–45 (italics in original).

rightist-oriented governments: leftist governments have systematically produced a higher rate of growth of the public sector of the economy, larger central government budgets, more income equalization, greater efforts to reduce unemployment, and more emphasis on education, public health, and social welfare spending than rightist governments. The evidence can be summarized in the following statement by Edward R. Tufte: "The single most important determinant of variations in macroeconomic performance from one industrialized democracy to another is the location on the left–right spectrum of the governing political party. Party platforms and political ideology set priorities and help decide policy."[5]

Although the overall conclusion is that left–right issue dimensions are real and pervasive and that they have major policy consequences, this does not mean they are the same in all countries. The distance between the political parties on the left–right spectrum appears to be the greatest in the United Kingdom, the Scandinavian countries, Finland, Iceland, Australia, and New Zealand, but most of the other countries also deserve a "high" rating on this dimension in table 8.1. Comparatively small differences are found in the United States, Canada, and Ireland; they are the only three with a "medium" rating. In none of our party systems is the left–right difference so small that it would be justified to conclude that the socioeconomic issue dimension is absent or of negligible importance.

THE RELIGIOUS DIMENSION

The second most important dimension, found in more than half of our twenty-two democracies, concerns party attitudes and policies toward religion and religious values. On this dimension,

5. Edward R. Tufte, *Political Control of the Economy* (Princeton, N.J.: Princeton University Press, 1978), p. 104.

too, a decline of ideology has occurred. In the continental European countries with mixed Catholic and Protestant populations and histories of Catholic–Protestant antagonism, interreligious tensions have largely disappeared and the two groups have even tended to unite politically. The Christian Democratic Union of postwar Germany was founded as a joint Catholic-Protestant party. In the Netherlands, the Catholic party and the two main Protestant parties presented a joint list in the 1977 parliamentary elections and merged into a single party organization soon thereafter. Only in Switzerland do the Christian Democrats remain an almost exclusively Catholic party. Moreover, both the explicitly religious parties and their anticlerical opponents have moderated their claims and counterclaims to a large extent. On the other hand, the religious and secular parties are still divided on a range of moral issues, such as questions of marriage and divorce, birth control, abortion, sex education, pornography, and so on. These issues have become especially prominent since the late 1960s.

Most of the party systems with an important religious cleavage can be found in continental Western Europe. Germany, Italy, Austria, Switzerland, Belgium, and the Netherlands all have major Christian Democratic parties. In France, the original Christian Democratic party of the Fourth Republic (MRP) has lapsed into insignificance as a separate party in the Fifth Republic, but the Gaullists now occupy the position of a conservative pro-church party. The end-of-ideology proposition with regard to the religious dimension appears to be disconfirmed by the emergence of Christian Democratic parties in all three Scandinavian countries and in Finland. Such parties were founded in Finland in 1958, in Sweden in 1964, and in Denmark in 1970. The Finnish and Danish, but not the Swedish, parties have achieved parliamentary representation. However, none of these parties can be regarded as "relevant" according to Sartori's criteria. Only the older Norwegian Christian People's party, established in 1933, has played a significant political role and has participated in several cabinets.[6]

Outside of Europe we find significant religious parties, indicative of the presence of a religious dimension in the party system, in Israel, Japan, and Australia. The National Religious party of Israel has been a crucial partner in almost all Israeli coalition cabinets in spite of its modest size, and it has been a highly effective advocate of orthodox religious policies. The Fair Play party of Japan is the political representative of the *Soka Gakkai* sect. Although its coalition potential is unclear, and will remain so as long as the Liberal Democratic party dominance lasts, its parliamentary strength qualifies it to be a significant party.

The reason why it can be argued that the Australian party system has a religious dimension is the role of the small Democratic Labor party. It is a Catholic offshoot from the large Australian Labor party, and "in composition, policies and goals it seems to resemble the European-type Christian Democratic parties."[7] The DLP has never been able to win seats in the House of Representatives and therefore has no coalition potential. On the other hand, it has helped the Liberals to win House seats by advising its supporters to mark Liberal candidates as their second preferences, and its senators have at times provided crucial support to Liberal–Country coalition cabinets in the federal chamber to which, as the constitutional crisis of 1975 shows, the cabinet can also be considered to be accountable (see chapter 6).

Finally, the absence of Canada from the countries with a significant religious dimension must be explained, because the Protestant–Catholic division is the best predictor of the voters' party choice. This difference between party supports is merely a

6. John T. S. Madeley, "Scandinavian Christian Democracy: Throwback or Portent?" *European Journal of Political Research* 5, no. 3 (September 1977):267–86.

7. Paul J. Duffy, "The Democratic Labor Party: Profile and Prospects," in Henry Mayer, ed., *Australian Politics: A Second Reader*, rev. ed. (Melbourne: Cheshire, 1971), p. 416.

survival of past conflicts and, as John Meisel emphasizes, religion is "of virtually no political importance in contemporary federal politics" in Canada.[8] Hence the Canadian case is a good illustration of the fact that issue dimensions in the party system cannot be inferred from the characteristics of party supporters.

THE CULTURAL-ETHNIC DIMENSION

In their developmental theory of cleavage structures and party systems, Seymour M. Lipset and Stein Rokkan identify four basic sources of party-system cleavages. These are, in addition to the socioeconomic and religious dimensions already discussed, cultural-ethnic cleavages and the divisions between rural-agrarian and urban-industrial interests.[9] The cultural-ethnic dimension appears much less frequently in the twenty-two party systems than the religious dimension, mainly because only four of our countries are ethnically and linguistically heterogeneous: Belgium, Canada, Switzerland, and Finland (see chapter 3).

The strongest cultural-ethnic dimension can be found in Belgium: it has become a sharp dividing line between the two communities and their parties. During the 1960s, three explicitly linguistic parties established themselves as important actors on the Belgian political scene: the *Volksunie* in Flanders, the Walloon Rally in Wallonia, and the Francophone Democratic Front in bilingual but mainly French-speaking Brussels. Subsequently, between 1968 and 1978, the three national parties—Christian Social, Socialist, and Liberal—split into autonomous Flemish and Francophone organizations. In Canada, the linguistic cleavage in the party system is less sharp: the Liberals are a broadly

8. John Meisel, *Cleavages, Parties and Values in Canada*, Sage Professional Papers in Contemporary Political Sociology, vol. 1, no. 06-003 (Beverly Hills, Calif.: Sage, 1974), p. 9.

9. Seymour Martin Lipset and Stein Rokkan, "Cleavage Structures, Party Systems, and Voter Alignments: An Introduction," in Seymour M. Lipset and Stein Rokkan, eds., *Party Systems and Voter Alignments: Cross-National Perspectives* (New York: Free Press, 1967), pp. 1–64.

based party and not the *exclusive* representative of Quebec and Francophone interests in federal politics, but they are virtually the *only* party spokesmen for these interests. The Swedish minority in Finland and the Swedish People's party are both quite small, but the party has been a very effective political actor and a very frequent partner in coalition governments.

Switzerland is often regarded as the multilingual society par excellence, but its party system reflects mainly religious and left–right differences, and cultural-ethnic issues are not salient at the national level. Even the "medium" rating on this dimension in table 8.1 may be too strong. The only other country with this rating is the United States. No American party has an exclusively ethnic base, but the Democrats have been much more representative of and sensitive to the interests of ethnic and racial minorities than the Republicans. Furthermore, to the extent that affirmative-action and other special minority programs have become controversial, the Democrats tend to defend and the Republicans to oppose them.

THE URBAN-RURAL DIMENSION

Differences between rural and urban areas occur in all democracies, but they constitute the source of issue dimensions in the party systems of only a few. Where agrarian parties are found, mainly in the Nordic countries, they have tended to become less exclusively rural and to appeal to urban electorates too, prompted by the decline of the rural population. A clear sign of this shift is that the Swedish, Norwegian, and Finnish agrarian parties all changed their names to "Center Party" between 1957 and 1965. The Danish Liberals and the Icelandic Progressives also originated as agrarian parties but now similarly try to portray themselves as center parties. The only other party system with an unambiguous urban-rural dimension can be found in Australia, where the Country party represents agrarian interests.

The two countries for which table 8.1 above indicates a weaker urban-rural issue dimension are Switzerland and the French Fourth Republic—both having parties that may be regarded as partly agrarian. The Swiss People's party is the new name of the old Peasants, Artisans, and Middle Class party. The French Peasants were a loosely organized group affiliated with the Independents in the national legislature of the Fourth Republic, but they lost most of their separate identity in the Fifth Republic.

THE DIMENSION OF REGIME SUPPORT

This dimension occurs in democracies as a result of the presence of important parties that oppose the democratic regime or, as in the case of the Gaullists during the French Fourth Republic, demand a drastic overhaul of the democratic form of government. From 1945 to 1980, the dimension of regime support was salient mainly in countries with sizable Communist parties: France, Italy, Finland, and Japan.

With regard to this dimension, too, a decline of ideology has developed. The trend toward "Eurocommunism" has entailed basic changes in Communist attitudes toward both democracy and foreign policy. For this reason, only one of the party systems in table 8.1 was given a "high" rating on this dimension: the French Fourth Republic, against which the Communists and Gaullists united in total opposition. The Fifth Republic, Italy, Finland, and Japan were judged to have only a weak dimension of regime support mainly because of the moderating of Communist attitudes during the second half of the 1945–80 period.

The only other country with a sizable Communist party is Iceland, but the Icelandic Communists may be said to have been Eurocommunists since 1938. At that time they joined with a Socialist faction to form a new party which, as the Icelandic political scientist Olafur R. Grimsson states, "would acknowledge the parliamentary road to power, adhere to an Icelandic form of socialism, and resign the [party's] membership in the Comintern, a position which reflected more the European 1970s than the late 1930s."[10]

THE FOREIGN POLICY DIMENSION

Eurocommunism also implies that the European Communist parties have undergone a fundamental shift in their traditionally pro-Soviet foreign policy preferences. The Italian Communists clearly exemplify such a shift. In France, however, the Communists have maintained their strict allegiance to the Soviet Union, and their Icelandic counterparts have been the main spokesmen against membership in NATO and the American military base near Reykjavik. The principal foreign policy issue in Japan is the American-Japanese Security Treaty, but the main cleavage is not between Communists and non-Communists but between the Liberal-Democratic party, joined by the small Democratic Socialist party, and the other parties. Finland is the only country with a large Communist party that does not have foreign policy as an issue dimension: Finnish neutralism with a slight pro-Soviet tilt is broadly supported by the Communist and non-Communist parties alike as well as by the government of the Soviet Union.

The French party system is characterized by a second foreign policy dimension that concerns the parties' attitudes toward European integration. It divides both the two main parties on the left, the pro-integration Socialists and the anti-integration Communists, and the two main parties on the right, the pro-integration Republicans and the anti-integration Gaullists. The same cleavage has appeared in the three new member states of the European Community—the United Kingdom, Ireland, and Denmark—as well as in Norway which, after a divisive referendum, declined to join. In these countries, the divisions were often more intense within some parties, particularly among British and

10. Olafur R. Grimsson, "Iceland: A Multilevel Coalition System," in Eric C. Browne and John Dreijmanis, eds., *Government Coalitions in Western Democracies* (New York: Longman, 1982), p. 145.

Norwegian Laborites, than between the parties, but there have also been clear interparty differences, such as between the British Labour party, on the one hand, and the Conservatives and Liberals, on the other, and between the Irish Labour party and the other two main parties of Ireland. Because these divisions may be only temporary—in Norway the referendum settled the matter—they are indicated as being of medium salience in table 8.1.

Another Irish foreign policy dimension is the split between Fianna Fail and Fine Gael on the Treaty of 1921. It is of mainly symbolic significance in contemporary Irish politics, but it does result in at least slightly different attitudes toward the Northern Ireland problem. A similar but much stronger nationalist-territorial dimension marks the party system of Israel. As Israeli political scientist Ofira Seliktar states, the debate is "between those who follow the maximalist territorial tradition of the Revisionists and those who adhere to the more moderate territorial demands of the Socialist-Zionist school."[11] This issue dimension has been especially salient since the occupation of Arab territories in 1967.

THE MATERIALIST VS. POSTMATERIALIST DIMENSION

One question prompted by the end-of-ideology theory is whether the ideological synthesis of "conservative socialism" represents the end of the ideological dialectic or merely a new dominant thesis which will be challenged by a new antithesis. Two elements of such an antithetical ideology have emerged as a reaction to conservative socialism in the 1960s and 1970s: participatory democracy and environmentalism. The former can be seen as a reaction to the impersonality, remoteness, and centralization of bureaucratic decision-making created by conservative socialism. The latter is a reaction against the economic-growth orientation of conservative socialism.

11. Ofira Seliktar, "Israel: Fragile Coalitions in a New Nation," in ibid., p. 295.

Both participatory democracy and environmentalism fit the cluster of values of what Inglehart terms "postmaterialism." Inglehart found that, especially among young middle-class people in Western democracies, a high priority is accorded to goals like "seeing that the people have more say in how things get decided at work and in their communities" and "giving the people more say in important government decisions." Moreover, in the richer nations the cluster of postmaterialist values also included the objective of "trying to make our cities and countryside more beautiful."[12]

Postmaterialism has not yet become the source of a new issue dimension in many party systems. The only examples are Norway and Sweden, where the Center parties have made a smooth transition from old-fashioned rural to modern environmentalist values, and the Netherlands, where two new parties, Democrats '66 and Radicals, have espoused participationist ideology. The limited impact of postmaterialism is not surprising because it is always difficult for a new issue dimension to become represented in an established party system. In addition, the postmaterialists are still only a small minority. In Inglehart's surveys of the nine countries of the European Community in the 1976–79 period, the average proportion of postmaterialist respondents was a meager 12 percent.[13] Another obstacle to a postmaterialist breakthrough in the party system is that the postmaterialist activists have tended to work through the leftist parties,

12. Ronald Inglehart, *The Silent Revolution: Changing Values and Political Styles among Western Publics* (Princeton, N.J.: Princeton University Press, 1977), pp. 40–50. The other postmaterialist values are much vaguer ("progress toward a less impersonal, more humane society" and "progress toward a society where ideas are more important than money") or not really new ("protecting freedom of speech").

13. Ronald Inglehart, "Post-Materialism in an Environment of Insecurity," *American Political Science Review* 75, no. 4 (December 1981):891. See also J. F. Pilat, "Democracy or Discontent? Ecologists in the European Electoral Arena," *Government and Opposition* 17, no. 2 (Spring 1982):222–33, and Ferdinand Müller-Rommel, "Ecology Parties in Western Europe," *West European Politics* 5, no. 1 (January 1982):68–74.

where their middle-class background has clashed with the traditional working-class orientation of those parties, and where the essentially conservative nature of environmentalist thinking is not easily reconcilable with the leftist self-image of progressivism.

ISSUE DIMENSIONS AND "FAMILIES" OF POLITICAL PARTIES

The number of issue dimensions in each country and the frequency of each dimension among the twenty-one countries are shown in the last column and in the bottom row of table 8.1; a dimension with a "medium" rating is counted as one-half of a full high-salience dimension. The most common dimensions are the socioeconomic one, present in all party systems, and the religious one, found in more than half. Next in importance are the urban-rural and foreign policy dimensions, each occurring in slightly over one-third of the party systems. The remaining three are much rarer. Only one country has a single interparty dimension: New Zealand. Two others, the United States and Ireland, have a score of 1.0 made up of two medium-salience dimensions. At the other extreme, the French Fourth Republic had both the largest number of issue dimensions, five, and the highest total score of 4.5.

The outstanding importance of the socioeconomic and religious dimensions is also manifested in the party system of the European Parliament, the legislature of the European Community, which was directly elected for the first time by the voters in the nine member states in 1979. The European Parliament contains six main political groups. Four of these represent true cross-national "families" of parties: the Christian democrats (officially called the European People's party), Socialists, Liberals, and Communists. In addition, there are two groups that are based on political convenience rather than unequivocal programmatic agreement. Of the four party families, the Communists are the

TABLE 8.2. Affiliation of Principal National Parties in Nine
Democracies with Party Groups in the European
Parliament, 1979

	Chr. Dem.	Soc.	Lib.	Comm.	Other	Totals
Belgium[a]	2	2	2		2	8
Denmark[b]		1	2	1	2	6
France[c]	1	1	1	1	1	5
Germany	1	1	1			3
Ireland	1	1			1	3
Italy	1	2	2	1		6
Luxembourg	1	1	1			3
Netherlands	1	1	1		1	4
United Kingdom		1	1		1	3
Total	8	11	11	3	8	41

[a]The Walloon Rally and Francophone Democratic Front are counted as a single party since they presented a joint list to the electors.
[b]The Danish Radicals are included in the Liberal category, although they were not successful in the 1979 election.
[c]Of the 25 candidates elected on the Union for French Democracy list, 17 joined the Liberals and 8 the Christian Democrats.

Source: Adapted from F. W. S.Craig and T. T. Mackie, Europe Votes 1: European Parliamentary Election Results 1979 (Chichester, Eng.: Parliamentary Research Services, 1980), pp. 147–51.

least important since they were elected only in France and Italy, and joined in parliament by one Danish politician elected, not on the Communist but on the radical leftist Socialist People's party ticket. The remaining three families—Christian Democrats, Socialists, and Liberals—reflect a party system based on the two dimensions of socioeconomic and religious issues.

It should also be pointed out that most of the significant parties (again according to Sartori's criteria) in the nine countries fit the four families of political parties. Table 8.2 summarizes this pattern. There are only eight important national parties that are not affiliated with one of these European parliamentary groups: the British and Danish Conservatives (allied in the "European Democratic" group), the Gaullists, the Irish Fianna Fail, the Danish Progress party (allied in the "European Progressive Democrats" group), the Dutch Democrats '66, and the Belgian linguistic parties. All of the others, more than four-fifths of the total, do fit the four-family pattern.

ISSUE DIMENSIONS AND COALITION THEORY

So far we have mainly tried to identify the relative *frequency* of the different dimensions. Can we also measure their relative *strength?* In particular, in party systems in which both of the most frequent dimensions are present, can we determine whether the socioeconomic or the religious dimension is the stronger one?

This question has received a full and satisfactory answer for the level of voting behavior. Socioeconomic status and religion (church affiliation and church attendance) have long been recognized as prime determinants of party choice. Comparative electoral research has also shown that socioeconomic status, or social class, is of universal importance in virtually all industrialized democracies, and that religion is often not important at all, such as in religiously homogeneous societies; however, when both factors play a role, religion tends to have a stronger influence on party choice. As Philip E. Converse points out, the general rule is that "religious differentiation intrudes on partisan political alignments in unexpectedly powerful degree wherever it conceivably can."[14] In the three democracies where social class, religion, and language are competing influences on party choice—Belgium, Canada, and Switzerland—religion and language are much more powerful predictors of voting behavior than class.[15]

At the beginning of this chapter, I warned that issue dimensions of party systems cannot simply be inferred from patterns of voting behavior. However, we have already found that socio-

14. Philip E. Converse, "Some Priority Variables in Comparative Electoral Research," in Richard Rose, ed., *Electoral Behavior: A Comparative Handbook* (New York: Free Press, 1974), p. 734.

15. Arend Lijphart, "Religious vs. Linguistic vs. Class Voting: The 'Crucial Experiment' of Comparing Belgium, Canada, South Africa, and Switzerland," *American Political Science Review* 73, no. 2 (June 1979):442–58.

economic issues constitute a significant dimension in all of our democracies, and it seems plausible to hypothesize that when this dimension competes with a religious one, the latter may be more powerful—in line with the findings of voting behavior research. How can we test this hypothesis?

The most suitable test is suggested by coalition theory. In chapter 4 we found that the policy-based theories have the best predictive ability: parties prefer to coalesce with other parties that have similar policy preferences. Hence we can also assume that when compatible coalitions can be formed along two different issue dimensions, parties will tend to choose the dimension that is most important to them. Figure 8.1 presents a typical situation in which such a choice has to be made and which therefore permits a test of the relative strength of the socioeconomic and religious dimensions: the party system of Luxembourg following the parliamentary elections of 1959. There are three parties that are potential coalition partners, none of which has a majority of parliamentary seats: two secular parties situated on the left and right of the socioeconomic dimension and a religious party with a center position on the socioeconomic dimension. There are four possible majority coalitions. The center–left and center–right coalitions indicate that the socioeconomic dimension is the dominant one, because they minimize the distance on this dimension in spite of a maximum difference on the religious dimension. The formation of the left–right coalition shows that the religious dimension predominates, because now the religious distance is minimized and the socioeconomic distance maximized. The left–center–right coalition is a grand coalition of all three parties and leaves the question of the relative strength of the two dimensions unanswered.

It would be desirable to apply this test to all thirteen party systems with a religious dimension in table 8.1 and for the entire period from 1945 to 1980, but two countries and many years in the other countries have to be excluded. The reason is that the party systems have to conform strictly to the model exemplified

FIGURE 8.1. Pattern of Potential Cabinet Coalitions in Luxembourg, 1959–64

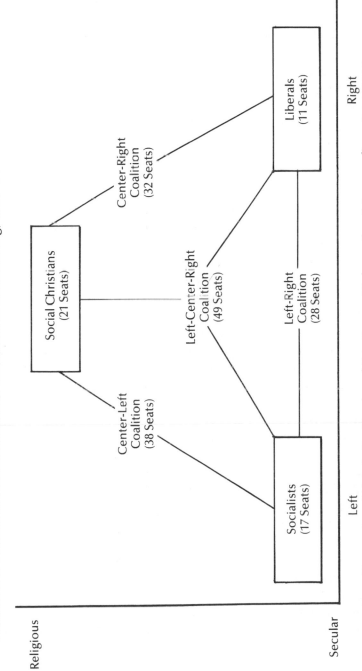

Religious

Social Christians
(21 Seats)

Center-Right
Coalition
(32 Seats)

Liberals
(11 Seats)

Left-Center-Right
Coalition
(49 Seats)

Center-Left
Coalition
(38 Seats)

Left-Right
Coalition
(28 Seats)

Socialists
(17 Seats)

Left

Right

Secular

Note: The number of seats in the Chamber of Deputies was 52; hence the minimum parliamentary support needed by a majority coalition cabinet was 27.

by Luxembourg in figure 8.1: (1) The party systems must have both a socioeconomic and a religious dimension, with the religious party in approximately the center of the left–right spectrum; this requirement excludes Australia, because the Democratic Labor party has never been able to win House seats, and also, for instance, Germany after 1972, when the Free Democrats, partly as a result of their close alliance with the Socialists during 1969–72, had moved to the center and could no longer be regarded as more rightist than the Christian Democrats. (2) There must not be a single party or a combination of parties belonging to the same grouping (secular left, secular right, or religious center) with a majority of parliamentary seats—rendering the formation of the majority coalitions shown in figure 8.1 unnecessary; this criterion excludes Japan, because in the period that the religious Fair Play party has been in parliament, from 1967 on, the Liberal Democrats, sometimes with the help of independents, have had absolute majorities. (3) The most important criterion mandated by the model of figure 8.1 is that both types of coalition must be numerically possible: either a center–left or a center–right coalition, or both, and a left–right coalition must be capable of being formed; this third criterion combined with the second one excludes rather long periods in the remaining eleven countries.

Table 8.3 shows the results of our test. Since we are interested in comparing the strengths of the socioeconomic and religious dimensions, only the left–right, center–left, and center–right coalitions are included in the table, and any minority left, center, or right cabinets, as well as any broad left–center–right coalitions, are omitted. The evidence shows that, contrary to our initial hypothesis derived from voting behavior research, the socioeconomic dimension is vastly more important than the religious one. Center–right and center–left coalitions together indicate that the socioeconomic dimension predominated, and they occurred 84 percent of the time under consideration. Left–right coalitions, indicating a dominant religious dimension, occurred

TABLE 8.3. Types of Government Coalitions in Eleven
Democracies, 1945–1980 (In Months)

	Left-Right	Center-Left	Center-Right	Totals
Austria	0	161	0	161
Belgium	62	27	61	150
France IV	0	0	23	23
France V	0	0	46	46
Germany	37	34	109	180
Israel	4	64	0	68
Italy	0	3	0	3
Luxembourg	60	0	129	189
Netherlands	0	48	22	70
Norway	0	0	78	78
Switzerland	0	0	72	72
All 11 democracies	163	337	540	1040
	(16%)	(32%)	(52%)	(100%)

Source: Based on data in Jean-Claude Colliard, *Les Régimes parlementaires contemporains* (Paris: Presses de la Fondation Nationale des Sciences Politiques, 1978), pp. 311–54; Eric C. Browne and John Dreijmanis, eds., *Government Coalitions in Western Democracies* (New York: Longman, 1982); and *Keesing's Contemporary Archives* (London: Keesing's Publications).

only 16 percent of the time. The ratio is more than 5 to 1. This pattern was quite stable during the 1945–80 period: the percentages were 86 and 14 percent in the first half of the period and 83 and 17 percent in the second half. It should also be noted that, in each country, the number of months of center–left and center–right coalitions is invariably greater than the number of months of left–center coalitions.

THE NUMBER OF PARTIES AND
THE NUMBER OF ISSUE DIMENSIONS

The final topic of this chapter is the relationship between the effective number of parties and the number of issue dimensions in the party system. There are two reasons to expect a strong link. First, when there are several dimensions of political conflict in a society, one would expect that a relatively large number of par-

TABLE 8.4. Effective Number of Parties and Number of Issue
Dimensions in 22 Democracies, 1945–1980

	Fewer than 3.0 parties	3.0 to 4.0 parties	More than 4.0 parties
1.0 or 1.5 dimensions	Canada (1.5) Ireland (1.0) New Zealand (1.0) United Kingdom (1.5) United States (1.0)		
2.0 or 2.5 dimensions	Australia (2.5) Austria (2.0) Germany (2.0)	Luxembourg (2.0) Sweden (2.5)	Denmark (2.5)
3.0 or more dimensions		Belgium (3.0) France V (3.5) Iceland (3.0) Italy (3.0) Japan (3.0) Norway (3.5)	Finland (3.5) France IV (4.5) Israel (3.0) Netherlands (3.0) Switzerland (3.0)

Note: The number of issue dimensions is shown in parentheses.

ties are needed to express all of these dimensions, unless they
happen to coincide with each other. Second, we have defined
issue dimensions in terms of differences between instead of within
parties. This means that, for instance, two-party systems cannot
accommodate as many issue dimensions as multiparty systems.

The coefficient of correlation between the effective number
of parties in the twenty-two democracies (table 7.3) and the
number of issue dimensions (table 8.1) is indeed a strong .75.
Table 8.4 shows the relationship in terms of where each regime
fits this pattern. As in previous tables, the effective number of
parties is trichotomized, and the number of issue dimensions is
also divided into three categories. Unfortunately, the latter threefold classification cannot be effected in such a way as to yield
categories with approximately equal numbers of countries. Partly
as a result of this, there are relatively many deviant cases, but
the majority of the countries are still on the expected diagonal.

It should also be noted that there are no extremely deviant cases. The average number of issue dimensions in party systems with relatively few parties is 1.6; in the intermediate category, this average is 2.9; and when there are many parties, the average increases to 3.2. The general rule is that the number of issue dimensions increases as the number of parties increases.

9 Electoral Systems: Majority and Plurality Methods vs. Proportional Representation

The sixth dimension on which the majoritarian and consensus models differ is a clear-cut one. The typical electoral system of majoritarian democracy is the single-member district plurality or majority system; consensus democracy typically uses proportional representation. The plurality and majority single-member district methods are a perfect reflection of majoritarian philosophy: the candidate supported by the largest number of voters wins, and all other voters remain unrepresented. Moreover, the party gaining a nation-wide majority or plurality of the votes will tend to be overrepresented in terms of parliamentary seats. In sharp contrast, the basic aim of proportional representation is to represent both majorities and minorities and, instead of over-representing or underrepresenting any parties, to translate votes into seats proportionally.

This chapter will first present a more detailed classification of the electoral systems used in our twenty-two democracies. It will then discuss the major theories concerning the relationship between electoral systems and party systems, and present the findings on the relationship in our set of countries between the electoral system and the effective number of parties. Finally, the different electoral systems will be compared with regard to their tendency to yield proportional or disproportional results, to reduce the effective number of parties in parliament, and to translate electoral pluralities into parliamentary majorities.

ELECTORAL FORMULAS

Although the dichotomy of proportional representatives vs. single-member district plurality and majority systems is indeed the most fundamental dividing line in the classification of electoral systems, we must make some additional important distinctions and develop a more refined typology.[1] Electoral systems may be described in terms of five dimensions: electoral formulas, district magnitudes, provisions for supplementary seats, electoral thresholds, and ballot structures.

Figure 9.1 presents a classification according to the first of these dimensions, the electoral formula. The classification is limited to the formulas used for the election of the first or only chambers in the twenty-two democracies in the 1945–80 period, and it is therefore not an exhaustive classification of all possible electoral formulas—or even of all formulas that have actually been used somewhere in the world. The first category of plurality and majority formulas can be subdivided into three more specific classes. The plurality formula is by far the simplest one: the candidate who receives the most votes, whether a majority or a plurality, is elected. Majority formulas require an absolute majority for election. One way to fulfill this requirement is to conduct a run-off second ballot between the top two candidates if none of the candidates in the first round of voting has received a majority of the votes. An example is the method used for the election of the president in the Fifth French Republic, but it is not used for legislative elections. The National Assembly in the

1. Thorough treatments of electoral systems are W. J. M. Mackenzie, *Free Elections: An Elementary Textbook* (London: Allen and Unwin, 1958); Enid Lakeman, *How Democracies Vote: A Study of Electoral Systems*, 4th ed. (London: Faber and Faber, 1974); and Dieter Nohlen, *Wahlsysteme der Welt: Daten und Analysen* (Munich: Piper, 1978).

FIGURE 9.1. A Classification of the Electoral Formulas for the
Election of the First or Only Chambers in 22
Democracies, 1945–1980

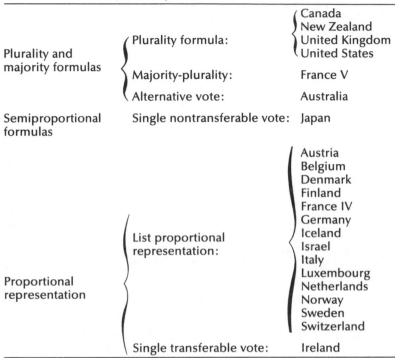

Plurality and majority formulas	Plurality formula:	Canada / New Zealand / United Kingdom / United States
	Majority-plurality:	France V
	Alternative vote:	Australia
Semiproportional formulas	Single nontransferable vote:	Japan
Proportional representation	List proportional representation:	Austria / Belgium / Denmark / Finland / France IV / Germany / Iceland / Israel / Italy / Luxembourg / Netherlands / Norway / Sweden / Switzerland
	Single transferable vote:	Ireland

Fifth Republic is elected by a mixed majority-plurality formula
in single-member districts: on the first ballot an absolute majority is required for election, but if no candidate wins a majority, a
plurality suffices on the second ballot. Candidates failing to win
a minimum percentage of the vote on the first ballot—12.5 percent since 1976–are barred from participating on the second ballot.

The alternative vote, used in Australia, is a true majority
formula. The voters are asked to indicate their first preference,
second preference, and so on among the candidates. If a candidate receives an absolute majority of the first preferences, he or

she is elected. If there is no such majority, the candidate with the lowest number of first preferences is dropped, and the ballots with this candidate as the first preference are transferred to the second preferences. This procedure is repeated by excluding the weakest candidate and redistributing the ballots in question to the next highest preferences in each stage of the counting, until a majority winner emerges.

Two main types of proportional representation must be distinguished. The most common form is the list system, used in a majority—14 out of 22—of our democratic regimes. There are minor variations in list formulas, but they all basically entail that the parties nominate lists of candidates in multimember districts, that the voters cast their ballots for one party list or the other, and that the seats are allocated to the party lists in proportion to the numbers of votes they have collected. List P.R. systems may be subdivided further according to the mathematical formula used to translate votes into seats. The most frequently applied method is the d'Hondt formula, which has a slight bias in favor of large parties as against small parties. The Sainte-Laguë method, used in Scandinavia, and the largest remainders method, used in Italy, in Israel for the 1951 through 1969 elections, and in some of the districts in the French Fourth Republic, are somewhat more favorable to the smaller parties.[2]

The other principal form of proportional representation is the single transferable vote. It differs from list P.R. in that the voters vote for individual candidates instead of for party lists. The ballot is similar to that of the alternative vote system: it contains the names of the candidates, and the voters are asked to rank-order these. The procedure for determining the winning candidates is slightly more complicated than in the alternative vote method. Two kinds of vote transfers take place: first, any surplus votes not needed by candidates who already have the minimum quota of votes required for election are transferred to

2. The complex French electoral law of 1951 also contained some majoritarian elements.

the next highest candidates; second, the weakest candidate is eliminated and his or her votes are transferred in the same way. If necessary, these steps are repeated until all of the available seats are filled. The single transferable vote is often praised because it combines the advantages of permitting votes for individual candidates and of yielding proportional results, but it is not used very frequently. The only instance in figure 9.1 is Ireland. The other major examples of its application are the Australian Senate and the unicameral legislature of Malta.

Most electoral formulas fit the two large categories of proportional representation and plurality-majority, but there are a few that fall in between. These semiproportional systems are used rarely, and the only example in our set of countries is Japan's single nontransferable vote. Each voter has one vote to be cast for a single candidate in a multimember district, and the candidates with the most votes are elected. The single nontransferable vote makes minority representation possible—in a five-member district, for instance, about one-fifth of the votes cast for one minority candidate guarantees election—but it does not guarantee overall proportional or close to proportional results.

OTHER DIMENSIONS OF ELECTORAL SYSTEMS

In addition to the electoral formula, there are four other dimensions along which electoral systems may differ:

1. District magnitude. The magnitude of an electoral district denotes the number of candidates to be elected in the district. It should not be confused with the geographical size of the district or with the number of voters in it. Plurality and majority formulas may be applied in both single-member and multi-member districts, but single-member districts have become the rule for national legislative elections. Proportional and semiproportional formulas require multimember districts, ranging from two-member districts to a single nation-wide district from which all members of parliament are elected. District magnitude has a very strong impact on the degree of proportionality that P.R. systems can attain. For instance, a party representing a 10 percent minority is unlikely to win a seat in a five-member district but will be successful in a ten-member district. Two-member districts can therefore hardly be regarded as compatible with the principle of proportionality; conversely, a nation-wide district is, all other factors being equal, optimal for a proportional translation of votes into seats. The magnitude of districts is much more important in this respect than the specific P.R. formula—d'Hondt, Sainte-Laguë, or largest remainders—that is applied in each district.

Among the sixteen proportional and semiproportional systems, there are three examples of nation-wide districts; Israel, the Netherlands, and Germany since 1957. The German electoral system is often described as a mixed plurality-proportional one, but is an unbalanced mixture that is almost entirely proportional as far as the overall allocation of seats is concerned. Three countries—Italy, Finland, and Luxembourg—have large average district magnitudes of more than ten members per district. The remaining countries have smaller districts.

2. *Supplementary seats.* In order to correct the deviations from proportionality caused by small district magnitudes, a number of seats may be reserved in a national pool (or in a few large-area pools) and allocated to the underrepresented parties. Especially if relatively many seats are awarded on this basis, proportionality can be closely approximated. Electoral systems with such provisions for supplementary seats are those of Austria, Denmark, Iceland, and Sweden since 1970.

3. *Electoral thresholds.* Nation-wide districts and supplementary seats tend to maximize proportionality and to facilitate the representation of even very small parties. In order not to make it too easy for small parties to win election, all countries with

nation-wide districts or supplementary seats have instituted minimum thresholds for representation, defined in terms of a minimum number of seats won at the district level and/or a minimum percentage of the total national vote. These percentages may be relatively low and hence innocuous, as the 1 percent threshold in Israel and the .67 percent threshold in the Netherlands. But when they reach 4 or 5 percent, as in Sweden and Germany respectively, they constitute formidable barriers to small minorities.

4. Ballot structure. Douglas W. Rae suggests a final dimension of electoral systems which he calls the "ballot structure." Ballots can be categorical or ordinal. Categorical ballots "require that the voter give his mandate to [one or more candidates of] a single party," while ordinal ballots allow the voter to "divide his mandate among parties or among candidates of different parties."[3]This dimension overlaps the electoral formula and district magnitude dimensions to a large extent. Single-member district plurality systems and the single nontransferable vote have, by definition, categorical ballot structures. The alternative vote and the single transferable vote are ordinal, and so is the French majority-plurality system whenever a second ballot is required, which tends to be the case in most districts. The only electoral system that can belong to either type is list P.R., but it is rarely ordinal. Only in Switzerland and Luxembourg can the voter divide his or her vote among more than one list. In the other list P.R. systems, the voters are sometimes allowed to express preferences among candidates of the same list but they cannot vote for more than one party list or for candidates of different parties.

ELECTORAL SYSTEMS AND PARTY SYSTEMS

A well-known proposition in comparative politics is that single-member district plurality systems favor two-party systems, as in-

3. Douglas W. Rae, *The Political Consequences of Electoral Laws*, rev. ed. (New Haven, Conn.: Yale University Press, 1971), pp. 17, 126.

dicated in figure 7.1 above; Maurice Duverger, writing in 1951, calls this proposition one that approximates "a true sociological law." Conversely, proportional representation and two-ballot systems encourage multipartism. Duverger explains the differential effects of the electoral system in terms of "mechanical" and "psychological" factors. The mechanical effect of the single-member district plurality system is that all but the two strongest parties are severely underrepresented, since they tend to lose in each district; the British Liberals, continually the disadvantaged third party in the postwar era, are a good example. The psychological factor reinforces the mechanical one: "the electors soon realize that their votes are wasted if they continue to give them to the third party: whence their natural tendency to transfer their vote to the less evil of its two adversaries."[4] Proportional representation does not have such a restraining influence on third and other weak parties and hence it freely allows the emergence and persistence of multiparty systems.

Several political scientists have gone further and have argued that proportional representation, as a result of its encouragement of the proliferation of parties, is a grave danger to the survival of democracy—in line with the second majoritarian proposition shown in figure 7.1. In his famous book *Democracy or Anarchy?*, first published in 1941, Ferdinand A. Hermens held proportional representation responsible for the failure of the Weimar Republic and the rise of Hilter: "P.R. was an essential factor in the breakdown of German democracy."[5] This explanation may have some validity for the case of Weimar, but it does not stand up as a general proposition. As discussed in chapter 7, in our set of countries with long records of reasonably stable democracy, the majority have multiparty systems. Similarly, most

4. Maurice Duverger, *Political Parties: Their Organization and Activity in the Modern State*, trans. Barbara and Robert North (New York: Wiley, 1963), pp. 217, 226.
5. F. A. Hermens, *Democracy or Anarchy? A Study of Proportional Representation* (New York: Johnson Reprint Corporation, 1972), p. 293.

of these countries have used proportional representation for a long time. Hermens's dire warning about P.R. is obviously exaggerated.

Nevertheless, the link between electoral and party systems—Duverger's "true sociological law"—is indeed a strong one. Its rationale is reinforced by the fact that, as Duverger recognized, the relationship is mutual. Single-member district plurality systems favor the persistence of two dominant parties, but, conversely, two-party systems are also favorable to the retention of the plurality method: it gives the two major parties the great advantage of protecting their dominance against attacks by third parties. For the same reason, proportional representation is likely to be retained by multiparty systems, because for most of the parties a switch to the plurality method would be extremely hazardous.

Of our twenty-two democratic regimes, only two deviate from Duverger's law. Duverger would have predicted that the four single-member district plurality systems—Canada, New Zealand, the United Kingdom, and the United States—would produce two-party systems. Canada with its two-and-a-half party system is the only exception. For all fifteen P.R. systems and for the French Fifth Republic, he would have predicted multipartism. Duverger did not include the Japanese semiproportional system and the Australian alternative vote in his analysis, but the logic of his law leads to a prediction of multipartism, since neither contains a strong deterrent to relatively weak parties. All eighteen non-plurality systems should therefore have multiparty systems; in fact, seventeen of them do, and Austria is the only deviant case. The Austrian two-party system reflects a plural society which happens to consist of two large subsocieties, Catholic and Socialist. This case shows that proportional representation should not be said to *cause*, but only to *allow* multipartism. The exceptional Canadian case is usually explained in terms of Canada's cultural and regional diversity, which is sufficiently strong to overcome the deterrent effect of the plurality system.

Rae has contributed a number of significant refinements to the study of the links between electoral and party systems. Different electoral systems have different impacts on party systems but, Rae emphasizes, they also have important effects in common.[6] In particular, *all* electoral systems, not just the plurality and majority systems, tend to overrepresent the larger parties and underrepresent the smaller ones. Three important aspects of this tendency must be distinguished: (1) All electoral systems tend to yield disproportional results. (2) All electoral systems tend to reduce the effective number of parliamentary parties compared with the effective number of electoral parties. (3) All electoral systems can, to use Rae's term, "manufacture" a parliamentary majority for parties that have not received majority support from the voters. On the other hand, all three tendencies are considerably stronger in plurality and majority than in proportional representation systems. These relationships, as well as the link between electoral systems and the effective number of parties, will be discussed in greater detail in the remainder of this chapter.

ELECTORAL SYSTEMS AND THE EFFECTIVE NUMBER OF PARTIES

Duverger's law distinguishes merely between two-party and multiparty systems, but its logic allows a more refined formulation: the more "permissive" an electoral system is, the larger one can expect the effective number of parties to be. The effective number of parties should therefore be low in plurality systems, somewhat higher in majority systems, higher still in semiproportional systems, and highest under proportional representation. The first column of table 9.1 repeats the information on the effective number of parliamentary parties contained in table 7.3 above, but it arranges the countries according to their electoral systems.

6. Rae, *The Political Consequences of Electoral Laws*, pp. 67–129.

TABLE 9.1. Effective Numbers of Parliamentary and Electoral Parties, Reductions in the Effective Numbers of Parties, and Deviations from Proportionality in 22 Democracies, Classified by Electoral System, 1945–1980

	Effective number of parliamentary parties	Effective number of electoral parties	Reduction in number of parties (%)	Index of disproportionality (%)
Plurality and majority:				
Canada	2.4	3.1	20.6	8.1
New Zealand	2.0	2.4	16.7	6.3
United Kingdom	2.1	2.6	17.4	6.2
United States	1.9	2.1	6.3	5.6
France V	3.3	4.8	30.7	12.3
Australia	2.5	2.8	7.2	5.6
Single nontransferable vote:				
Japan	3.1	3.8	18.7	4.2
Proportional representation:				
Austria	2.2	2.4	7.5	2.0
Belgium	3.7	4.1	10.0	2.2
Denmark	4.3	4.5	4.5	0.9
Finland	5.0	5.4	7.5	1.6
France IV	4.9	5.1	4.1	2.8
Germany	2.6	2.9	9.3	2.1
Iceland	3.5	3.7	5.2	3.0
Israel	4.7	5.0	6.6	1.1
Italy	3.5	3.9	11.1	2.2
Luxembourg	3.3	3.6	9.4	3.2
Netherlands	4.9	5.2	6.7	1.1
Norway	3.2	3.9	16.9	3.1
Sweden	3.2	3.4	5.5	1.2
Switzerland	5.0	5.4	7.4	1.5
Ireland	2.8	3.1	9.6	2.4

Source: Based on data in Thomas T. Mackie and Richard Rose, *The International Almanac of Electoral History* (London: Macmillan, 1974); *European Journal of Political Research*, vols. 2–9, no. 3 (September 1974–81); and John F. Bibby, Thomas E. Mann, and Norman J. Arnstein, *Vital Statistics on Congress, 1980* (Washington, D.C.: American Enterprise Institute, 1980), pp. 6–7.

Within the general category of plurality and majority systems, the four plurality regimes are listed first; among the fifteen P.R. systems, the one single transferable vote system (Ireland) is at the bottom of the table.

The evidence generally supports the refined form of Duverger's law. The greatest contrast is between plurality and P.R. systems: the average effective number of parties in the former is 2.1 and in the latter 3.8—almost twice as many. The number of parties in the French Fifth Republic, in Australia, and in the Japanese semiproportional system—3.3, 2.5, and 3.1, respectively—fall in between the two extremes. It should be noted, however, that, contrary to our expectations, the number is actually a bit lower in the semiproportional Japanese system than in the majoritarian French one.

We might also expect that within the general class of P.R. systems, the more permissive forms—that is, those with nationwide districts or supplementary seats—would have more parties than the less permissive systems. This hypothesis must be rejected. There is virtually no difference between the two. As we shall see shortly, the former do yield more proportional results than the latter, but this difference does not affect the number of parties.

DEGREES OF DISPROPORTIONALITY

Except under the most unusual circumstances, it is impossible for any electoral system to yield exactly proportional results. Parliaments have a given number of seats, and the seat shares given to the different parties can almost never be made mathematically equal to their vote shares. Hence it is an unsurprising tautology to state that all electoral systems tend to yield disproportional results. The more interesting generalization, however, is that all electoral systems achieve considerably less proportionality than what *is* mathematically possible.

The two commonly used indices of disproportionality are

those proposed by Douglas Rae (I) and by John Loosemore and Victor J. Hanby (D).[7] On the basis of the result of a given election, Rae calculates the absolute differences between the vote percentages (v_i) and seat percentages (s_i) of all parties (n) that have received at least one-half percent of the total votes, and uses the average of these percentages as his index of disproportionality:

$$I = \frac{1}{n} \sum_{i=1}^{n} \left| v_i - s_i \right|$$

Loosemore and Hanby focus on the total amount of deviation from proportionality that a given election produces: the difference between the vote and seat percentages of all of the overrepresented parties together—which is, of course, the same as the total difference between the vote and seat shares of the underrepresented parties:

$$D = \frac{1}{2} \sum_{i=1}^{n} \left| v_i - s_i \right|$$

In order to calculate their index, Loosemore and Hanby add the absolute values of all of the vote-seat share differences, like Rae, but then divide by 2, instead of Rae's division by the number of parties. Hence, except in a strict two-party system, the Hanby-Loosemore index will produce higher values than Rae's.

Both indices have serious weaknesses. Rae's index is overly sensitive to the presence of very small parties. For instance, a party receiving 1 percent of the vote is highly unlikely to receive 2 percent or more of the seats; a much more probable outcome is that it will not get any seats at all. The maximum vote-seat share deviation for this party will therefore be 1.0 percent. Since the

7. Ibid., pp. 84–86; John Loosemore and Victor J. Hanby, "The Theoretical Limits of Maximum Distortion: Some Analytic Expressions for Electoral Systems," *British Journal of Political Science* 1, no. 4 (October 1971):467–77.

average deviation found by Rae in 116 elections in twenty countries is 2.39 percent, the presence of any party with between 0.5 and about 2 percent of the vote will decrease the average index for an election. Since such small parties typically occur in P.R. systems, Rae's index overstates the proportionality attained by P.R.[8]

The Loosemore-Hanby index is much too sensitive to the number of parties participating in an election. Imagine, for example, an election in which all parties receive seat shares that deviate only 1 percent from their vote shares—a highly proportional result. If there are two parties, the Loosemore-Hanby index is 1.0. With ten parties, however, the index assumes the very high value of 5.0. Since there is a strong relationship between P.R. and multipartism, the Loosemore-Hanby index tends to understate the proportionality of P.R. systems.

This critique also suggests an alternative index which avoids the shortcomings of the Rae and Loosemore-Hanby indices. It should average the vote-seat share differences of the larger parties only and/or of the same number of parties in different elections and countries. Our index uses both of these remedies: it is the average vote-seat share deviation of the two largest parties in each election. How these large parties fare is a good reflection of the overall proportionality of an election result.

The fourth column of table 9.1 shows that all electoral systems yield results that are to some extent disproportional, but the degree of disproportionality ranges from a low average of only 0.9 percent in Denmark to a very high average of 12.3 percent in the Fifth Republic. The average index of disproportionality for the six plurality and majority systems is 7.4 percent, and for the four plurality systems 6.6 percent. The 15 P.R. systems have an average index of only 2.0 percent. Evidently, although P.R. systems do not yield perfect proportionality, they perform considerably better in this respect than nonproportional sys-

8. Another practical problem of the Rae index is that election statistics frequently do not give the votes and seats of small parties separately but lump them together as the votes and seats won by "other parties."

tems. The semiproportional Japanese system has an index of disproportionality of 4.2 percent—roughly in between the 2.0 and 7.4 percent of the two major categories.

A closer look at the indices of disproportionality of the fifteen P.R. systems in table 9.1 reveals that, on the one hand, all of the values are relatively low—not even one of them has an index that comes close to the lowest of the plurality and majority systems—but that, on the other hand, there is still considerable variation. Some of this variation can be explained in terms of nationwide districts and supplementary seats. The democracies using these devices—Austria, Denmark, Germany from 1957 on, Iceland, Israel, the Netherlands, and Sweden since the 1970 election—have an index of disproportionality of only 1.5 percent, compared with 2.4 percent for the other P.R. systems. Beyond this, it becomes very difficult to determine the exact effects of different P.R. formulas, varying district magnitudes, the use of supplementary seats, and electoral threshold levels; we simply have too few cases to test all of these variables.

Fortunately, we can find some evidence concerning the effects of these variables in those countries that have introduced slight changes in their P.R. systems while leaving all or most of the other dimensions of their electoral systems unchanged. Israel moved from the less proportional d'Hondt formula to the more proportional largest remainders method between the 1949 and 1951 elections, but returned to d'Hondt by 1973; the average degree of disproportionality was 2.2 percent in the 1949, 1973, and 1977 elections, compared with only 0.5 percent in the elections from 1951 through 1969. Norway changed from d'Hondt to the more proportional Sainte-Laguë formula in 1953; its average index of disproportionality fell from 5.4 percent to 2.4 percent. Sweden adopted the same change in 1952, and its index went down from 2.4 percent in 1948 to 1.2 percent in the elections from 1952 through 1968. The adoption of a supplementary seat system in 1970 resulted in a further drop to 0.8 percent in the four elections of the 1970s.

Similar evidence on the effect of changing district magnitudes can be found in electoral reforms adopted by Iceland, Germany, and Austria. Until 1959, Iceland had very small districts with an average magnitude of 1.5 seats. In fact, only about half of the district seats were at stake in list P.R. multimember districts, and the other half in plurality single-member districts; this electoral system can be regarded as primarily a proportional one only by virtue of the supplementary seats intended, in the words of the Icelandic constitution, for "equalization between the parties so that each of them shall be represented as nearly as possible in proportion to the number of votes obtained in the general election."[9] The single-member districts were abolished in 1959, and the average district magnitude was increased from 1.5 to 6.1 seats. The index of disproportionality fell from 4.9 percent in the elections before the change to 1.7 percent after. In Germany, the large districts coinciding with the *Länder* were merged into a nation-wide district before the 1957 election; disproportionality decreased from 3.5 to 1.7 percent, although the electoral threshold was reinforced at the same time. The new Austrian electoral law of 1971 decreased the number of districts from 25 to 9, entailing a commensurate increase in average district magnitude, and designated two instead of four areas for the allocation of supplementary seats. Both measures were designed to, and did, achieve greater proportionality: the index fell from an average of 2.5 percent in the 1945–70 elections to 0.6 percent since 1971.

REDUCING THE EFFECTIVE NUMBER OF PARTIES

The disproportionality characteristic of all electoral systems tends to favor the larger parties and to discriminate against the smaller ones. As a result, all electoral systems tend to reduce the effective number of parties. The first and second columns of table 9.1 show that in every country the average number of electoral par-

9. Article 31D.

ties is greater than the average number of parties in parliament. The averages of the percentage reduction in each election are given in the third column. The highest and lowest values, 30.7 and 4.1 percent, both occur in France: in the Fifth and Fourth Republics, respectively.

Although the reduction in the effective number of parties is a general effect of electoral laws, it is a much stronger tendency in plurality and majority systems than in P.R. systems: the respective averages are 16.5 and 8.1 percent. The single nontransferable vote in Japan results in a high 18.7 percent reduction. As expected, in the general category of P.R. systems, those with nationwide districts or supplementary seats do not reduce the effective number of parties as much as the others, 6.0 percent compared with 9.9 percent.

The reduction in the number of parties is mainly a function of the disproportionality of the electoral system. A comparison of the third and fourth columns of table 9.1 reveals that the index of disproportionality is closely related to the decrease in the effective number of parties; the correlation coefficient is .82. It should be noted that this is a stronger relationship than that between the index of disproportionality and the effective number of parliamentary parties, which is a somewhat less impressive but, of course, still strong − .51.

MANUFACTURED MAJORITIES

The tendency of electoral systems to yield disproportional results favoring the large parties becomes especially important when parties that fail to get a majority of the votes are awarded a majority of the seats. This makes it possible to form single-party majority cabinets—one of the hallmarks of majoritarian democracy. Rae calls such majorities "manufactured," that is, artificially created by the electoral system. Manufactured majorities may be contrasted with earned majorities, when a party wins majorities of both votes and seats, and natural minorities, when

TABLE 9.2. Manufactured Majorities, Earned Majorities, and Natural Minorities in Three Types of Electoral Systems, 1945–1980

	Manuf. maj. (%)	Earned maj. (%)	Natural min. (%)	Totals (%)
Plurality and majority systems (6 countries)	45	25	29	100 (75)
Single nontransferable vote (Japan)	40	20	40	100 (15)
Proportional representation (15 countries)	7	4	89	100 (149)
All elections in 22 democracies	21	12	67	100 (239)

Source: Based on data in Thomas T. Mackie and Richard Rose, *The International Almanac of Electoral History* (London: Macmillan, 1974); *European Journal of Political Research*, vols. 2–9, no. 3 (September 1974–81); and John F. Bibby, Thomas E. Mann, and Norman J. Arnstein, *Vital Statistics on Congress, 1980* (Washington, D.C.: American Enterprise Institute, 1980), pp. 6–7.

no party wins a majority of either votes or seats.[10] An extremely rare fourth possibility, artificial minorities, when there is a majority vote winner that does not obtain a seat majority, occurred only once in the 239 elections in our countries between 1945 and 1980: in the 1954 Australian election, the Labor party was defeated even though it won 50.1 percent of the popular vote. (This one exceptional case will be included in our category of natural minorities.) Majorities were manufactured in as many as 50 elections, and were earned in only 28 elections. The remaining 161 elections produced natural minorities.

Table 9.2 presents the average incidence of manufactured and earned majorities and of natural minorities in the three main types of electoral systems. All three are capable of creating majorities where none are created by the voters, but this capacity is especially strong in the plurality and majority systems—closely

10. Rae, *The Political Consequences of Electoral Laws*, pp. 74–77.

followed by the Japanese semiproportional system, which has frequently manufactured majorities for the Liberal Democrats. The clearest cases are Great Britain and New Zealand, our principal examples of Westminster democracy. In the 1945–80 period, ten out of eleven British elections (91 percent) manufactured single-party majorities—and made single-party majority cabinets possible. One election, held in February 1974, did not produce a majority. In postwar Britain, therefore, not one parliamentary majority was actually earned. All twelve elections in New Zealand produced majority winners: 9 of the 12 majorities (75 percent) were manufactured, and only 3 were earned. In the other four plurality and majority systems, manufactured majorities have also occurred, but less frequently: in 46 percent of the elections in Canada, 33 percent in Australia, 17 percent in the United States, and 17 percent in the French Fifth Republic. The average for the six countries is 46 percent.

In contrast, proportional representation very rarely produces manufactured majorities. They have occurred in only five of the fifteen P.R. systems—Austria, Belgium, Ireland, Italy, and Norway—and the average incidence in the fifteen countries is only 7 percent. It is especially in this respect that proportional representation is a vital element of consensus democracy, and plurality and majority systems, particularly the single-member district plurality system, of majoritarian democracy.

Division of Power: The Federal-Unitary and Centralized-Decentralized Contrasts

10

The seventh difference between the majoritarian and consensus models of democracy concerns the division of power between the central government and the governments at lower levels. In all democracies, power is necessarily divided to some extent between the central and noncentral governments, but it is a highly one-sided division in majoritarian democracy. In order to maintain majority rule, the majority must control not only the central government apparatus but also all noncentral, potentially competing, governments. Majoritarian government is therefore unitary and centralized. The consensus model is inspired by the opposite aim. Its methods are federalism and decentralization. Federalism means a constitutionally guaranteed division of power between the central government and the governments of the member units or component units of the federation (states, provinces, cantons, and *Länder*). It is usually accompanied by decentralization, that is, substantial autonomy for the members of the federation. Only six of our twenty-two democratic regimes—the United States, Canada, West Germany, Switzerland, Austria, and Australia—are federal, but federalism is neither a necessary nor a sufficient condition for decentralization. As we shall see, decentralized power may also occur in formally unitary states.

This chapter will first discuss the distinctive characteristics of federalism, with a special emphasis on the representation of the constituent units in the federal chamber of the central legislature and on the extent to which federations are in fact decentralized. Next, it will analyze federalism as a means of giving autonomy to minority groups in plural societies, and the special form of federalism usually referred to as corporate or nonterritorial federalism. The final topic will be a preliminary examination of the relationship between federalism and decentralization, on the one hand, and the elements of consensus democracy discussed earlier, on the other hand.

FEDERALISM

A variety of definitions of federalism may be found in the literature on this subject, but there is broad agreement on its primary characteristic: a guaranteed division of power between central and regional governments. William H. Riker's authoritative definition reads as follows: "Federalism is a political organization in which the activities of government are divided between regional governments and a central government in such a way that each kind of government has some activities on which it makes final decisions."[1] One aspect of this definition that deserves emphasis and to which I shall return later in this chapter, is that the component units are referred to as "regional" governments. This is in accordance with the conventional view: federalism is usually described as a spatial or territorial division of power in which the component units are geographically defined.

In addition to the primary federal principle of a central-regional division of power, five secondary characteristics of federalism can be identified: a written constitution, bicameralism, the right of the component units to be involved in the process of amending the federal constitution but to change their own con-

1. William H. Riker, "Federalism," in Fred I. Greenstein and Nelson W. Polsby, eds., *Handbook of Political Science, Vol. 5: Governmental Institutions and Processes* (Reading, Mass.: Addison-Wesley, 1975), p. 101.

stitutions unilaterally, equal or disproportionally strong representation of the smaller component units in the federal chamber, and decentralized government.

First, the requirement of a written constitution follows logically from the primary federal principle: the division of power has to be specified, and both the central and regional governments need a firm guarantee that their allotted powers cannot be taken away. A written compact is a necessary, but of course not sufficient, method to specify these respective powers and guarantees. The next chapter will discuss the contrast between written and unwritten constitutions in more detail. Here it should be noted that all of the six federal regimes have written constitutions, whereas most but not all of the sixteen unitary regimes do.

Second, the legislatures of federal systems typically consist of two chambers, one representing the people at large and the other the component units of the federation. As discussed in chapter 6, of the parliaments in our twenty-two democratic regimes, fourteen are bicameral and eight are unicameral. All of the unicameral legislatures occur in unitary states, while bicameralism is found in six federal and eight unitary states. In other words, all of our federal systems have bicameral parliaments.

The third characteristic concerns the division of constituent power. It is often argued that it is in the nature of federal constitutions that they may not be changed without the consent of the component units. This consent may take the form of approval by the federal chamber and/or approval by at least a majority of the legislatures of or referendums in the component units. The only exception in our six federations is Austria, where the constitution can be amended by a two-thirds majority of the first chamber without the additional requirement of either federal chamber or Länder approval. In all six federations, the component units do have their own constitutions, which they can amend freely within certain limits set by the federal constitution. Hence, as Carl J. Friedrich states, the component units in a federation "retain . . . a certain amount of the constituent power and therefore characteristically order autonomously their own internal exercise of power over those matters which the [federal] constitution leaves to them."[2]

One of the alleged advantages of the independent constituent power of the component units of a federation is that it gives them the opportunity to experiment with different forms of government. Such experimentation, if successful, can be beneficial both for the other members of the federation and for the federal government. In practice, however, we find almost complete isomorphism both between the federal and component units' governmental forms and between those of the component units in each country. With regard to the choice of presidential or parliamentary systems and of the electoral system, for instance, the United States is solidly presidential—the governors serving as "presidents" at the state level—and majoritarian. A few noteworthy exceptions in the other countries may be mentioned. The Australian House of Representatives and the lower houses of the Australian states are all elected by the alternative vote, except one: Tasmania uses proportional representation (the single transferable vote). Proportional representation is the norm both at the national and cantonal levels in Switzerland, but a few, mainly small, cantons use majority methods. All of the German *Länder* have parliamentary systems, but in Bavaria the prime minister cannot be dismissed by a vote of no confidence. In Switzerland, the cantons deviate from the hybrid parliamentary-presidential system at the federal level, but they are similar to each other in having popularly elected collegial executives—basically a presidential form of government. It is symptomatic that the drafters of the constitution of the new canton of Jura, which formally came into being in 1979, discussed the British and German ex-

2. Carl J. Friedrich, *Limited Government: A Comparison* (Englewood Cliffs, N.J.: Prentice-Hall, 1974), p. 21. See also Ivo D. Duchacek, *Comparative Federalism: The Territorial Dimension of Politics* (New York: Holt, Rinehart, and Winston, 1970), pp. 230–31.

amples of a parliamentary system, but that in the end they stuck to "accepted Swiss norms."[3]

OVERREPRESENTATION AND DECENTRALIZATION

The fourth of the subsidiary characteristics of federalism is that the smaller component units are overrepresented in the federal chamber: their share of legislative seats exceeds their share of the population. The maximum extension of this principle is equality of representation regardless of the component units' population. We find such parity in the federal chambers of the United States and Switzerland (two representatives per state or canton) and Australia (ten representatives per state). The German *Bundesrat* and the Canadian Senate are examples of federal chambers in which the component units are not equally represented but in which the smaller units are overrepresented and the larger ones underrepresented. The Austrian *Bundesrat* is an exception, as its membership is roughly proportional to the population of the *Länder* rather than giving special representation to the smaller *Länder*.[4]

Table 10.1 presents the degree of overrepresentation of the smaller units of the six federations in a more precise way—in terms of the degree of inequality of representation caused by the favorable treatment of the small units. It shows the percentage of the membership of the federal chamber that represents the most favorably represented 5, 10, 25, and 50 percent of the population. The best-represented people are those in the smallest component units of the federation. The following example illustrates how

3. Hanspeter Tschaeni, "Constitutional Change in Swiss Cantons: An Assessment of a Recent Phenomenon," *Publius* 12, no. 1 (Winter 1982): 116.

4. A partial exception to parity in Australia is that the Australian Capital Territory and the Northern Territory each has two senators. In Canada, the degree of overrepresentation does not correspond entirely to size; for instance, the least favorably represented province is not the largest, Ontario, but the third largest, British Columbia.

Table 10.1. Inequality of Representation in Six Federal Chambers, ca. 1980

	Percentages of seats held by given percentages of the most favorably represented voters				Gini Index of Ine-quality
	5%	10%	25%	50%	
United States	28.2	39.5	60.6	82.9	.50
Switzerland	26.7	38.9	60.4	81.1	.48
Australia	21.3	30.4	55.3	75.7	.39
Germany[a]	20.1	31.5	50.7	73.1	.36
Canada	18.9	31.2	48.5	69.2	.31
Austria	6.9	12.8	28.2	53.2	.05

[a]Excluding West Berlin

Source: Based on data in The Europa Year Book 1982: A World Survey (London: Europa Publications, 1982).

these percentages are calculated. Assume that the smallest and best represented state in a federation has 6 percent of the total population and 10 out of 100 seats in the federal chamber, and that the second smallest and second best represented state has 8 percent of the population and also 10 out of 100 federal chamber seats. Then the best represented 10 percent of the total population are the 6 percent in the smallest state plus half of the people in the second smallest state. Together, these 10 percent of the people have 15 percent of the seats in the federal chamber.

The inequality in the above illustration is very minor compared with the actual inequalities that we find in most of the federal chambers. The United States is the most extreme case: the most favorably represented 5 percent of the people, living in the smallest states, have 28.2 percent of the representation in the Senate; one-fourth of the best represented voters have a comfortable majority of 60.6 percent; and exactly half of them elect an overwhelming majority of almost 83 senators. The percentages for Switzerland are close to the American ones, and the Swiss Council of States can therefore be said to be almost as "malapportioned" as the United States Senate. Australia, Germany, and Canada are intermediate cases, but the inequalities are still substantial. The Austrian *Bundesrat* is the only federal chamber in which the degree of overrepresentation is so slight that it can almost be regarded as a proportionally apportioned house.

The Gini Index of Inequality is a summary measure of the degree of inequality. It can range from zero when there is complete equality—the Austrian index of .05 is close to this point—to a theoretical maximum approximating 1.00 when the most favorably represented unit has all of the seats in the federal chamber and the others get none. In the United States, if the state with the smallest population, Alaska, elected all 100 senators, the Gini Index would be .998. The actual index of .50 for the United States is exactly halfway between these extremes. The Swiss index of .48 follows closely, and those for the next three federal chambers are all still quite high, ranging between .31 and .39.

Two other aspects of table 10.1 deserve special emphasis. One is that the degree of minority overrepresentation in five of the six federations, excluding Austria, is so strong that one-fourth of the most favorably represented people have more than or, in the Canadian case, almost half of the representation in the federal chamber. Because of this characteristic, chapter 6 classified these five legislatures under the label of incongruent bicameralism. Second, it should be noted that the four legislatures that are the most incongruently bicameral—the American, Swiss, Australian, and German parliaments—are also those that were called strongly bicameral in chapter 6 because their two chambers are symmetrical or only moderately asymmetrical as far as their relative powers are concerned. Canadian bicameralism is incongruent, although less so than in the other four federations, but extremely asymmetrical, and Austrian bicameralism is the weakest, because it is both congruent and extremely asymmetrical.

The final characteristic of federalism is decentralized government. One of the foremost experts on federalism, Daniel J. Elazar, has objected to the term *decentralization* because it implies the existence of a central government that has the power to decentralize, and "the government that can decentralize can recentralize if it so desires. Hence, in decentralized systems the diffusion of power is actually a matter of grace, not right." The term that Elazar prefers is *non-centralization*, denoting a system in which "power is so diffused that it cannot legitimately be centralized or concentrated without breaking the structure and spirit of the constitution."[5]

The problem with Elazar's alternative term is that it is virtually synonymous with the primary federal principle of a guaranteed central-regional division of power, which logically implies that the power of the component units cannot be taken away without their consent. Noncentralization does not require that the noncentral governments' inalienable share of power be very extensive. Hence we do need a term to describe the actual division of power, and the degree of centralization or decentralization can serve this purpose, as long as we are careful to avoid the implication of a unitary system in which the central government is potentially all-powerful. In other words, there can be both centralized and decentralized federations and, similarly, centralized and decentralized unitary states. In practice, as we shall see, federalism and decentralization tend to go together.

How can we measure the degree of centralization-decentralization? A common approach is to look at how extensive central and noncentral government activities are, measured in terms of their expenditures and revenues. Since expenditures and revenues are, if not in balance, at least in rough correspondence with each other, they can be used interchangeably. However, if we are interested in the noncentral governments' strength vis-à-vis the central government, it is theoretically more attractive to focus on their resources. Here we face the additional problem of how to measure central government grants to noncentral governments, which together with noncentral taxes are the most important components of noncentral government resources. It makes

5. Daniel J. Elazar, "Federalism vs. Decentralization: The Drift from Authenticity," *Publius* 6, no. 4 (Fall 1976): 13.

sense to exclude conditional or restricted transfers, since these are spent for purposes mandated by the central government. But even unrestricted grants do not necessarily mean that the noncentral government is given a free hand. As Douglas E. Ashford points out, they are frequently "not functions of the strength of local governments, but a measure of the central governments' ability to predict how the funds will be used."[6]

The most appropriate measure of centralization therefore entails a comparison of central and noncentral taxation. Noncentral tax revenues are defined as (1) taxes collected by the noncentral governments for themselves and (2) additional rates imposed on the taxes of the central government as well as shares of particular taxes collected by the central government accruing *automatically* to noncentral governments. Transfers of central government tax receipts to noncentral governments are specifically excluded. Moreover, all social security taxes are excluded.[7] Table 10.2 is based on this definition. It shows the percentage share of the central government's taxes in our twenty-one countries in the 1970s. The countries are listed in decreasing order of centralization. The Netherlands is the most centralized country: 98 percent of all taxes are the central government's. Switzerland is at the bottom of the list: here the central government claims considerably less than half, 41 percent, of all taxes.

The unitary and federal countries are listed in separate columns, and it is immediately clear from the table that there is a strong relationship between federalism and decentralization and between unitarism and centralization. The average degree of centralization of the fifteen unitary states is 83 percent, and of the six federal states 58 percent. There are some notable excep-

6. Douglas E. Ashford, "Territorial Politics and Equality: Decentralization in the Modern State," *Political Studies* 27, no. 1 (March 1979): 82.

7. Several alternative centralization indices are discussed in Wallace E. Oates, *Fiscal Federalism* (New York: Harcourt, Brace, Jovanovich, 1972), pp. 195–213. See also D. G. Davies, *International Comparisons of Tax Structures in Federal and Unitary Countries*, Research Monograph no. 16 (Canberra, Centre for Research on Federal Financial Relations, Australian National University, 1976).

TABLE 10.2.   Government Centralization in 15 Unitary and 6
Federal Regimes, Measured by the Central
Government's Share of Total Central and
Noncentral Tax Receipts, 1970s

Unitary	Federal	Central government's tax share (%)
Netherlands		98
Israel		96
Italy		96
Belgium		93
New Zealand		93
Ireland		92
France		88
United Kingdom		87
Iceland		83
Luxembourg		82
	Australia	80
Denmark		71
Finland		70
	Austria	70
Norway		70
Japan		65
Sweden		62
	United States	57
	Germany	51
	Canada	50
	Switzerland	41

Note: For most countries, the years covered are 1972, 1973, 1975, 1977, 1978, and 1979.

Source: Based on data in Organisation for Economic Co-operation and Development, *Revenue Statistics of OECD Member Countries, 1965–1980* (Paris, 1981), pp. 178–209; *Statistisk Årbog 1981* (Copenhagen, 1981); Johannes Nordal and Valdimar Kristinsson, eds., *Iceland, 874–1974* (Reykjavik: Central Bank of Iceland, 1975), pp. 248–55; and personal communication from Emanuel Gutmann (June 17, 1982).

tions, such as the relatively centralized Australian federation and the relatively decentralized but unitary Nordic countries and Japan. The figures in table 10.2 pertain to the 1970s. For all six federations and eleven of the fifteen unitary states (excluding France, Iceland, Israel, and Luxembourg), the relevant statistics for 1955 are also available. These show that, from 1955 to 1979, the degree of centralization in the federal systems declined from 69 to 58 percent, but that in the eleven unitary systems it remained unchanged at 82 percent.[8] In other words, during the approximate quarter of a century since the mid-1950s, the contrast between federal and unitary states has become more pronounced.

CONGRUENT AND INCONGRUENT FEDERALISM

One purpose of federalism may be to give autonomy to particular groups such as religious and ethnic minorities, particularly if they form distinct subsocieties in a plural society. In order to analyze this function of federalism it is useful to make a distinction between congruent and incongruent federalism, as suggested by Charles D. Tarlton. Congruent federations are composed of territorial units with a social and cultural character that is similar in each of the units and in the federation as a whole. In a perfectly congruent federal system, the component units are "miniature reflections of the important aspects of the whole federal system." Conversely, incongruent federations have units with social and cultural compositions that are different from each other and from the country as a whole.[9] Another way of expressing

8. Calculated from data in Organisation for Economic Co-operation and Development, Long-Term Trends in Tax Revenues of OECD Member Countries, 1955–1980 (Paris, 1981), p. 21. See also G. Warren Nutter, Growth of Government in the West (Washington, D.C.: American Enterprise Institute, 1978), pp. 90–94.

9. Charles D. Tarlton, "Symmetry and Asymmetry as Elements of Federalism: A Theoretical Speculation," Journal of Politics 27, no. 4 (November 1965): 868. It should be noted that Tarlton uses the terms symmetry and asymmetry instead of congruence and incongruence. Because the former pair of terms is

this difference is to compare the political boundaries between the component units of the federation and the social boundaries between groups like religious and ethnic minorities. In incongruent federations, these boundaries tend to coincide, but they tend to cut across each other in congruent federal systems.

If the political boundaries are drawn in such a way that they approximate the social boundaries, the heterogeneity in the federal state as a whole is transformed into a high degree of homogeneity at the level of the component units. In other words, incongruent federalism can make a plural or semiplural society less plural by creating relatively homogeneous smaller areas. The degree of congruence in federal systems can be determined by comparing the heterogeneity in the country as a whole with the weighted average heterogeneity or homogeneity of the component units (that is, weighted by the population sizes of the component units). The best measure for this purpose is the Rae-Taylor index of fragmentation.[10] It can vary between 0 and 1: the value is 0 for a completely homogeneous society and 1 for a hypothetical extreme case of a plural society where each individual belongs to a different group. For a society that is evenly divided into two groups, the index is .50; if one group has 80 percent and the other 20 percent of the population, the index is .32.

Table 10.3 presents the indices of fragmentation for the six federations and for semifederal Belgium as well as the comparable weighted averages for their component units. The indices are based on the division of the societies into ethnic or religious groups. The ethnic groups are those of Belgium (Dutch-speakers,

most often used to describe different distributions of power—for instance, between the two chambers of bicameral legislatures—it is less confusing to use the latter pair of terms to characterize different compositions of two or more entities. Congruence and incongruence in federalism have a meaning that is analogous to congruence and incongruence in bicameralism, as used in chapter 6.

10. Douglas W. Rae and Michael Taylor, *The Analysis of Political Cleavages* (New Haven, Conn.: Yale University Press, 1970), pp. 22–44. This index is closely related to the Laakso-Taagepera index of the effective number of parties (see chapter 7, note 9).

TABLE 10.3. Ethnic and Religious Fragmentation in Seven
Federations, ca. 1970–1980

	Whole country	Weighted average in subunits	Decrease in fragmentation (%)	Number of units in federation
Congruent federations				
Australia	.58	.58	0	8
Austria	.56	.55	2	9
Germany	.56	.49	13	11
United States	.29	.28	6	51
Incongruent federations				
Belgium	.53	.14	74	3
Canada	.54	.33	38	12
Switzerland	.53	.34	36	26

Source: Based on census data for Australia (1971), Belgium (1981), Canada (1976),
Germany (1970), Switzerland (1970), and the United States (1980); election data
for Austria (1979); and estimates by Wilfried Dewachter (personal communica-
tions, June 11 and June 30, 1982) and the author.

French-speakers, and others), Canada (English-speakers, French-
speakers, and others), and Switzerland (German-, French-, Ital-
ian-, Romansh-speakers, and others). For the United States, the
following groups, officially recognized in the 1980 census, were
taken into consideration: (1) whites, (2) blacks, (3) American In-
dian, Eskimo, and Aleut, (4) Asian and Pacific Islander, and (5)
others. In Australia and Germany, religious fragmentation into
Protestants, Catholics, and others was computed. The divisions
of overwhelmingly Roman Catholic Austria are those of religios-
ity and ideology. They cannot be measured with census data but
they do correspond closely with the political cleavages dividing
Austria's four political parties (Socialists, Catholics, Liberals, and
Communists); for this reason the 1979 parliamentary election results were used.

The table shows that there are two clearly different patterns.
In Australia, Austria, Germany, and the United States, the fragmentation at the level of the component units is not much lower

than at the national level. The largest decrease from the national to the subunit level is only 13 percent in the case of Germany, due to the relative concentration of Protestants in the North and Catholics in the South. The federalism of these four countries is therefore mainly congruent. In the other three countries, the federal division has the effect of creating component units that are considerably more homogeneous than the society as a whole; these federations approximate the incongruent model. In Switzerland, there is considerably less linguistic diversity in the cantons than at the national level; the Swiss federation has four official languages, but most of the cantons can be officially unilingual. The Francophone minority of Canada is mainly concentrated in Quebec, but Ontario and New Brunswick also contain large numbers of French-speakers. Two of the three new regions created by the federalizing process in Belgium—Flanders and Wallonia—are almost completely homogeneous with regard to language, and they are also officially unilingual; only the smallest region, the capital city of Brussels, is bilingual both in fact and in law. As a result, Belgium has the largest reduction in fragmentation from the national to the regional level.

One possible explanation for the two contrasting patterns of table 10.3 is that it is easier to create homogeneous units in a heterogeneous society if these units can be very small and consequently if there are relatively many of them. For instance, the creation of the small homogeneously French-speaking canton of Jura, carved out of mainly German-speaking Berne in 1979, increased Swiss linguistic homogeneity at the cantonal level. Hence we could expect federations with many component units to be more incongruent than those divided into few units. Table 10.3 lists the number of component units of the seven federations, including not only the regular member units but also special areas like the District of Columbia, the Australian Capital Territory, and West Berlin. It is clear that this explanation has to be rejected. The average number of units in the congruent federations is actually greater than in the incongruent ones. Moreover, the federal system with the fewest component units, Belgium, has the largest decrease in fragmentation.

The main explanation, of course, is the degree of geographical concentration of the religious and ethnic communities. They are intermixed in the four congruent federations, whereas they are much more, albeit not completely, concentrated in distinct areas of the incongruent federations.

CORPORATE FEDERALISM

The conclusion of the previous section prompts the question of whether it may be possible to give autonomy to geographically interspersed groups by means of a federalism that is not defined exclusively in spatial-geographic terms. Most of the experts on federalism reject such a broadened concept of federalism, but a deviant minority has emphasized its theoretical and practical importance. Friedrich refers to nonterritorial federalism as "corporate" federalism, and he has forcefully called attention to the corporately federal proposals made by Otto Bauer and Karl Renner for the solution of the nationalities problem of the Austro-Hungarian Empire. Their key idea was that each individual should be able to declare to which nationality he or she wished to belong, and that these nationalities should then become autonomous nonterritorial cultural communities.

The first practical application of the Bauer-Renner proposals occurred in Estonia in 1925. Cultural minorities of a given minimum size were given the right to establish their own schools and cultural institutions, governed by elected councils with legislative and taxing powers. The jurisdiction of these cultural councils was defined in terms of membership in a cultural community regardless of geographical residence. The Russian and Swedish minorities did not set up such cultural councils, mainly because they were geographically concentrated and could therefore use local self-governmental institutions. However, the more scattered German and Jewish minorities did make use of the opportunity of the new law, and their cultural councils soon proved successful: "the Estonian Government was able to claim, with every justification, that it had found an exemplary solution to the problem of its minorities."[11]

Another example of corporate federalism may be found in the 1960 constitution of Cyprus. In Friedrich's words, "the federalism chosen for Cyprus was what might be called 'corporate federalism'—a scheme once proposed for the solution of the nationality problems of the Hapsburg Empire and afterward adopted in Estonia."[12] Because the residential patterns of the Greek majority and the Turkish minority were at that time highly intermixed, a regular territorial federalism could not be instituted. Instead, the two ethnic segments were given a great deal of autonomy by means of two separately elected communal chambers with exclusive legislative powers over religious, educational, cultural and personal status matters, and separate municipal councils in the five largest towns of the island.

As discussed in chapter 2, Belgium is the most recent example of corporate federalism. The two cultural councils for Dutch-speakers and French-speakers are akin to the communal chambers of Cyprus. What is especially interesting in the Belgian case is that federalization since 1970 has simultaneously taken territorial and corporate forms. The country is divided into the three regions of Flanders, Wallonia, and Brussels, but also into a Dutch-speaking community (comprising both the geographically defined area of Flanders and the corporately defined group of Dutch-speakers in Brussels) and a French-speaking community (comprising both the area of Wallonia and the Francophone

11. Georg von Rauch, The Baltic States—Estonia, Latvia and Lithuania: The Years of Independence, 1917–1940, trans. Gerald Onn (Berkeley: University of California Press, 1974), p. 142.

12. Carl J. Friedrich, Trends of Federalism in Theory and Practice (New York: Praeger, 1968), p. 124. Corporate federalism should not be confused with "corporatism," a term referring to various arrangements linking the government, labor unions, business, and the economy. See Philippe C. Schmitter, "Still the Century of Corporatism?", Review of Politics 36, no. 1 (January 1974): 85–131.

Bruxellois). As a result, as Martin O. Heisler states, "for some purposes, Belgium [can] be thought of as a federal entity consisting of three units, while for other purposes it is comprised of only two."[13] The three-unit federation, or semifederation, is a territorial one, while the two-unit federation is mainly corporate.

The final extension of the concept of federalism is to apply it to arrangements whereby autonomy is granted to private organizations that represent distinct groups in a society. Especially in Austria, Belgium, and the Netherlands, the central governments have long recognized and subsidized various associations, especially in the fields of education, health care, and the mass media, that were established by the major religious and ideological subsocieties—Catholics, Socialists, Liberals, and, in the Netherlands, Protestants. This type of federalism may be called informal corporate federalism or, as Robert A. Dahl has suggested, "sociological federalism."[14] It is worth noting that Belgium has been a particularly active laboratory for federal experiments, and that it was sociologically federal long before it began to adopt corporate and territorial federalism.

FEDERALISM, DECENTRALIZATION, AND CONSENSUS DEMOCRACY

What is the relationship between federalism and decentralization, on the one hand, and the other elements of consensus democracy, on the other hand? Previous chapters have found strong links between the type of cabinet, cabinet durability, the effective number of parties, the number of issue dimensions, and the electoral system. Federalism and decentralization are hardly related to this set of characteristics. For instance, the adjusted percent-

13. Martin O. Heisler, "Managing Ethnic Conflict in Belgium," *Annals of the American Academy of Political and Social Science* 433 (September 1977): 42.

14. Quoted in Sidney Verba, "Some Dilemmas in Comparative Research," *World Politics* 20, no. 1 (October 1967): 126.

age of time during which the countries have been governed by minimal winning coalitions (see table 4.2) is actually a bit higher on the average in federal than in unitary states—67 and 63 percent, respectively—contrary to the expected link. The average effective number of parties (see table 7.3) is also unexpectedly smaller in the six full federations, 2.8 parties, than in unitary states, 3.6 parties. Similarly, the correlation coefficient between the centralization indices of table 10.2 and the usual type of cabinets is an insignificant .03, and the correlation between centralization and the effective number of parties is .10—which is not only weak but also the opposite of the negative correlation to be expected. One problem could be that the high centralization indices of the Netherlands and Belgium (98 and 93 percent) do not do justice to the sociological federalism of these countries. If we arbitrarily lower these indices to the average for all federal and unitary states (76 percent), the two correlation indices become .11 and − .03 respectively—obviously still not showing very significant connections.

On the other hand, there is a close relationship with the type of legislature. As chapter 6 showed, all four countries with strong bicameralism—Australia, Germany, Switzerland, and the United States—are federal. These same four countries are also among the most decentralized systems: their average centralization is 57 percent compared with 80 percent in the other countries. These patterns among the different elements of majoritarian and consensus democracy will be explored further in the final chapter.

Constitutions: The Sovereignty of The Majority vs. Minority Rights

11

The eighth and last of the differences between the majoritarian and consensus models concerns the presence or absence of explicit restraints on the legislative power of parliamentary majorities. Is there a constitution serving as a "higher law" that is binding on parliament and that cannot be changed by a a regular parliamentary majority, or is parliament—that is, the majority in parliament—the supreme and sovereign lawmaker? This difference is traditionally analyzed in terms of the contrast between "written" and "unwritten" constitutions. It entails three important criteria that will be examined in greater detail in this chapter. The first, but least important, is the literal difference between a written constitution as a single document embodying the nation's highest law and an unwritten constitution that is merely a collection of important laws and customs. The second criterion concerns the procedures for amending the constitution: do they constitute a significant limitation on the parliamentary majority or not? Third, in cases of potential conflict between the constitution and an ordinary law, who is the interpreter of the constitution: parliament itself—again meaning the majority in parliament—or a body such as a court or a special constitutional council outside and independent of parliament?

WRITTEN AND UNWRITTEN CONSTITUTIONS

There are two reasons why the literal distinction between written and unwritten constitutions is relatively unimportant. One is that almost all of the constitutions in the world are written, and that unwritten ones are extremely rare. In our set of twenty-two democratic regimes we find only three with unwritten constitutions: those of Great Britain and New Zealand, the two prime examples of majoritarian democracy discussed in chapter 1, and of Israel. The absence of a written constitution in Britain and New Zealand is often explained in terms of their strong consensus on fundamental political norms, which render a formal constitution superfluous. The opposite explanation applies to the Israeli case. As Leonard J. Fein states, Israel has tried but failed to adopt a written constitution because "on a number of central questions—most notably, the relationship of religion to the State— the societal consensus was insufficient."[1] These disagreements have been solved by an agreement to disagree, while on other fundamental matters the consensus has been strong enough to allow the country to be run without a formal constitution, as in Britain and New Zealand.

Second, from the perspective of the fundamental contrast between the majoritarian and consensus models of democracy, it is more relevant to determine whether the constitution, written or unwritten, imposes significant restraints on the majority than to ask whether it is written or not. If it is a single document, explicitly designated as the nation's highest law, the parliamentary majority may feel morally bound to respect it to a greater degree than if it is merely a more or less amorphous collection of basic laws and customs without even a clear agreement on what exactly is and what is not part of the unwritten constitution. But in terms of their formal binding force, usually also backed by

1. Leonard J. Fein, *Politics in Israel* (Boston: Little, Brown, 1967), pp. 165–66.

TABLE 11.1.   Three Types of Procedures for Constitutional
Amendment in 22 Democratic Regimes

Pure majority rule	Approval by referendum	Minority veto
Iceland	Denmark	Australia
Israel	France IV	Austria
New Zealand	France V	Belgium
Sweden	Ireland	Canada
United Kingdom	Italy	Finland
		Germany
		Japan
		Luxembourg
		Netherlands
		Norway
		Switzerland
		United States

moral authority, written and unwritten constitutions may not differ
a great deal, as the next two sections will show.

CONSTITUTIONAL AMENDMENT
AND MINORITY VETO

Constitutional amendment may take many different forms, but
this variety can be reduced to three basic types. Changes in constitutions may have to be approved by special majorities, by a
popular referendum, or merely by a regular parliamentary majority. Table 11.1 classifies the twenty-two democratic regimes in
these three categories. The differences among these types are often
also described under the labels of "rigid" and "flexible" constitutions, according to the degree of difficulty in amending them.[2]
    1. The type of rule for constitutional amendment that con-
forms most closely to the consensus model of democracy is the
requirement of approval by a special majority—which entails

2. Ivo D. Duchacek, *Power Maps: Comparative Politics of Constitutions*
(Santa Barbara, Calif.: ABC-Clio, 1973), pp. 210–14.

the right of a minority of a given minimum size to exercise a veto power. The simplest and most common procedure embodying the minority veto is the need for an extraordinary majority—usually two-thirds—in parliament. Approval by majority vote in both houses of incongruently bicameral parliaments also implies a minority veto, since certain minorities are overrepresented in the second chamber.

As an alternative or an addition to minority veto at the national parliamentary level, the approval of subnational bodies like cantons or states, whether by legislative action or by referendum, may be required. In Switzerland, for example, constitutional amendments must be approved by a majority of the cantons—which gives the smallest cantons, with less than 20 percent of the total Swiss population, a potential veto. This rule may be strengthened further by stipulating not just a regular but a special majority of the subnational organs, as in the United States, where the three-fourths requirement means that the thirteen smallest states, with less than 5 percent of the population, can block a constitutional amendment. As table 11.1 shows, most of our twenty-two democratic regimes have relatively rigid constitutions with some kind of minority veto for constitutional amendment.

2. The second type of rule for constitutional change is approval by a national referendum. It could be argued that, unless a special majority of the voters have to give their approval, a referendum is merely a majoritarian instrument: the majority in parliament proposes an amendment, which is then accepted by a popular majority. This interpretation overlooks the possibility offered by a referendum that a committed minority may organize a strong campaign against the amendment. Hence, it seems justified to assign the requirement of a referendum to an intermediate category between the more majoritarian and more consensual types of amendment rules.

Of the five democracies in this category, Denmark and Ireland are straightforward examples. The other three are more complicated because their constitutions offer a choice of methods for constitutional amendment. The French Fifth Republic may serve as an illustration. The last article of its constitution states that amendments require the approval of either the two legislative chambers and a referendum, or a three-fifths majority of a joint session of the legislature.[3] In addition, President Charles de Gaulle's decision in 1962 to circumvent parliament and to submit a proposed amendment directly to a referendum, overwhelmingly approved by the voters, established this method as a third procedure for constitutional amendment. All cases in which alternative methods can be used are classified according to the more majoritarian or flexible option, because it is usually the parliamentary majority—or, as in France, the president elected by a popular majority—that decides which option shall be used.

3. The remaining five countries belong to the category of pure majority rule: their constitutions are completely flexible and can be changed by normal parliamentary majorities. The three regimes with unwritten constitutions automatically qualify for this type. The Swedish and Icelandic written constitutions can be amended by two successive majority decisions between which a parliamentary election has to be held. In principle, the function of such an intervening election is the equivalent of a referendum: it gives the voters a chance to elect legislators who will vote against the proposal for constitutional amendment approved by the previous legislature. In practice, constitutional questions of this kind hardly ever affect election campaigns, and intervening elections can therefore not be considered a real restraint on majority rule.

JUDICIAL REVIEW

One can argue that a written and rigid constitution is still not a sufficient restraint on parliamentary majorities, unless there is

3. Article 89.

an independent body that decides whether laws are in conformity with the constitution. If parliament itself is the judge of the constitutionality of its own laws, it can easily be tempted to resolve any doubts in its own favor. The remedy that is usually advocated is to give the courts or a special constitutional council the power of judicial review—that is, the power to test the constitutionality of laws passed by the national legislature.

In the famous *Marbury v. Madison* decision (1803), which established judicial review in the United States, Chief Justice John Marshall argued that the presence of a written constitution and an independent judiciary logically implied the Supreme Court's power of judicial review: the court, faced with an incompatibility between the Constitution and an ordinary law, had no choice but to apply the higher law and therefore to invalidate the law with a lower status. The strong appeal of this argument can also be seen in a comment by R. H. S. Crossman, a member of the British Labour cabinet responsible for the controversial 1968 immigration law denying entry into Britain to about a hundred thousand British subjects living in Kenya; he later said that this law "would have been declared unconstitutional in any country with a written constitution and a Supreme Court."[4]

Although the logic of Marshall's and Crossman's reasoning appears incontrovertible, it is not followed by all democratic regimes. Table 11.2 lists the regimes that do and that do not have judicial review. Among those that do not practice judicial review, we find, of course, the three countries with unwritten constitutions but also six that have written constitutions and high courts—which are explicitly denied the power of judicial review. In these countries, the parliaments are the ultimate guarantors of the constitution. The logic on which this alternative is based is that of democratic principle: such vitally important decisions as the conformity of law to the constitution should be made by the elected

4. Cited in Richard Rose, "A Model Democracy?", in Richard Rose, ed., *Lessons from America: An Exploration* (New York: Wiley, 1974), p. 138.

TABLE 11.2. Judicial Review and Minority Veto in 22
Democratic Regimes

		Judicial Review	
		No	Yes
Minority veto	No	France IV Israel New Zealand United Kingdom	Denmark France V Iceland Ireland Italy Sweden
	Yes	Belgium Finland Luxembourg Netherlands Switzerland	Australia Austria Canada Germany Japan Norway United States

representatives of the people rather than by an appointed and frequently quite unrepresentative judicial body.

Mainly as a compromise between these two contradictory logics, several countries entrust judicial review to special constitutional courts or councils instead of to the regular court systems. The regular courts may submit questions of constitutionality to the special constitutional court, but they may not decide such questions themselves. This type is called the centralized system of judicial review. It was first adopted in the Austrian First Republic and is now also used in Germany and Italy. The alternative, decentralized judicial review, in which all courts may consider the constitutionality of laws, is the more common system.[5]

5. Mauro Cappelletti, *Judicial Review in the Contemporary World* (Indianapolis: Bobbs-Merrill, 1971), pp. 45–68.

France was long considered the prime example of a country in which the principle of popular sovereignty was said to prevent any application of judicial review. The constitution of the Fifth Republic did set up a constitutional council, but at first this body served mainly to protect executive power against legislative encroachments; only the president, the prime minister, and the presidents of the two chambers were permitted to submit questions of constitutionality to the council. A constitutional amendment passed in 1974 also gave minorities in the legislature—sixty members of either chamber—the right to appeal to the constitutional council, and the council itself has strongly asserted its power of judicial review. Although the courts still cannot turn to the constitutional council, France must now be counted among the countries with at least some judicial review of the centralized kind.[6]

Among the democracies with decentralized systems of judicial review, there are wide differences in judicial activism. The United States, with its highly assertive judiciary, is at one extreme of this spectrum. The Scandinavian countries and Iceland are situated at the opposite end; in Mauro Cappelletti's words, their judges exercise the power of judicial review "with extreme prudence and moderation."[7] In Sweden, it was not until 1963 that the highest court asserted the right of judicial review, but it also stated that "the application thereof should be restrictive." When an entirely new constitution was adopted in 1974, no attempt was made to eliminate judicial review, but, significantly, it was not explicitly written into the new constitution either.[8]

6. See James Beardsley, "Constitutional Review in France," in Philip B. Kurland, ed., The Supreme Court Review, 1975 (Chicago: University of Chicago Press, 1976), pp. 189–259; and Barry Nicholas, "Fundamental Rights and Judicial Review in France," Public Law (Spring, Summer 1978), pp. 82–101, 155–77.

7. Cappelletti, Judicial Review in the Contemporary World, p. 59.

8. Constitutional Documents of Sweden (Stockholm: Swedish Riksdag, 1975), p. 28. For some of the intermediate cases—Australia, Canada, and Ireland—see Edward McWhinney, Judicial Review, 4th ed. (Toronto: University of Toronto Press, 1969).

FEDERALISM, JUDICIAL REVIEW, AND RIGID CONSTITUTIONS

How can we explain the incidence of judicial review? Donald P. Kommers has called for a systematic analysis "to find out whether judicial review is commonly associated with certain legal forms, political structures, modes of judicial organization, or constitutional values."[9] For our purposes, there are three important relationships that must be examined:

1. Judicial review entails a strong restraint on parliamentary majorities and is therefore a typical characteristic of consensus democracy. Similarly, a rigid constitution with a minority veto is antimajoritarian. Hence it makes sense to hypothesize that these two characteristics of consensus democracy would tend to go together. But table 11.2 above shows unambiguously that this hypothesis must be rejected: in eleven of our twenty-two democracies we find one of the two elements without the other.

2. The previous chapter indicated that a written constitution is one of the characteristics of federalism, as the division of power between the central and regional governments must be explicitly stipulated. One could argue further that there ought to be a neutral interpreter of this written constitution in order to prevent the central legislature from usurping the power reserved for the component units of the federation—which implies, of course, either a centralized or decentralized system of judicial review. A link between federalism and judicial review is indeed often asserted, but it is by no means a very strong link. As Kommers states, "the constitutions of the world do reveal the presence of judicial review as a constitutional principle in [most] federal systems of government," but it is also found "in numerous non-federal systems."[10] Five of our six federal states have judicial

9. Donald P. Kommers, "Comparative Judicial Review and Constitutional Politics," *World Politics* 27, no. 2 (January 1975): 293–94.

10. Donald P. Kommers, "Judicial Review: Its Influence Abroad," *Annals of the American Academy of Political and Social Science* 428 (November 1976): 62.

review—Switzerland is the one exception—but exactly half of the unitary states, eight out of sixteen, also have it.

3. Another look at table 11.2 reveals a much stronger and more interesting link with federalism: of the seven countries in the lower right-hand cell, characterized by both judicial review and minority veto, five are federal. These seven democracies have antimajoritarian constitutions in all three respects discussed in this chapter: written constitutions, minority veto, and judicial review. Five of the six federations belong to this group, but only two of the sixteen unitary states.

Chapters 6 and 10 found a relationship between federalism and strong bicameralism. We can now add the further link with antimajoritarian constitutions. We shall return to this pattern in the last chapter.

Referendums in Representative Democracies

12

The ninth characteristic of the Westminster model of democracy discussed in chapter 1 is that it is purely representative. The supremacy of the majority in parliament should not be contravened by direct popular participation, such as in a referendum. As chapter 2 argued, however, this ninth element of the Westminster model, unlike the other eight, does not distinguish it from the consensus model, which is also a model of representative democracy. Although referendums and other instruments of direct democracy are foreign to both majoritarian and consensual theory, they may occur to a certain degree in the practice of both types of democracy.

This chapter will discuss the various devices of direct democracy, with an emphasis on the one that has the greatest practical importance: the referendum. We shall examine the incidence and trends of the use of the referendum and try to explain its relatively infrequent, albeit increasing, application. Unfortunately, as we shall see, the question of why referendums occur much more frequently in some countries than in others cannot be answered satisfactorily.

FIGURE 12.1. The Pure Parliamentary System and Four
Elements of Direct Democracy

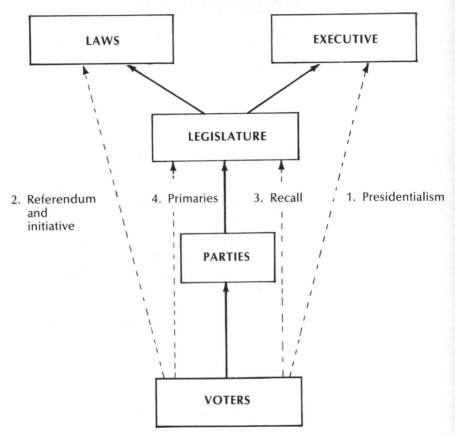

INSTRUMENTS OF DIRECT DEMOCRACY

Figure 12.1 outlines the principal institutions in a pure parliamentary system of government as well as the interrelationships
between these institutions (solid lines). The voters elect the
members of the legislature via the political parties, which nomi-

nate the candidates among whom the voters have to choose. The legislature selects the executive and makes the laws. The voters can therefore be said to have a direct influence over the legislature, although the parties play an intermediary role, but they influence the composition of the executive and the adoption of laws only indirectly, by way of their representatives in the legislature. Four methods (indicated by dotted lines in figure 12.1) have been proposed to strengthen the voters' influence and to make the democratic system more direct and less representative:

1. The most obvious way of democratizing the parliamentary model is to introduce the direct election of the executive by the voters instead of selection by the legislature. Since, as chapter 5 showed, popular election of the executive is incompatible with a system in which the executive is dependent on the legislature's confidence, this method of introducing a greater degree of direct democracy necessarily means a shift from parliamentary to presidential government. Parliamentarism and presidentialism can be seen as the two basic ways of replacing the monarch or other nondemocratic ruler and his cabinet with a democratically controlled executive. The parliamentary method, exemplified by the history of democratization in many European countries, is to make the cabinet responsible to the popularly elected legislature instead of to the monarch. The presidential method is more radical: it replaces the nondemocratic monarch with a democratically elected president. As Douglas Verney states, "by abolishing the Monarchy and substituting a President for the King and his Government, the Americans showed themselves to be truly revolutionary in outlook."[1]

It would be wrong, of course, to view the significance of presidentialism mainly in terms of its more democratic character in comparison with parliamentarism. Its primary importance lies in its impact on executive–legislative relations. Presidential government means separation of powers, and it increases the chances

1. Douglas V. Verney, *The Analysis of Political Systems* (London: Routledge and Kegan Paul, 1959), p. 43.

of a rough balance of power between the executive and the legislature (see chapter 5).

2. The second instrument for moving representative democracy in the direction of direct democracy is the popular referendum: instead of entrusting the power to make laws entirely to the legislature, the voters may also be called on to approve or reject proposed laws, which may be either regular laws on constitutional amendments. The voters' influence is strengthened a great deal if they are allowed not only to vote on propositions originating in the legislature or the executive but also to propose laws on their own initiative—that is, the initiative of a given minimum of the electorate. The referendum by itself entails a very modest step toward direct democracy but, combined with the initiative, it becomes a giant step.

3. One of Jean Jacques Rousseau's complaints about representative democracy was that representatives, once elected, cannot be controlled by the voters: "The English people thinks itself free, but is badly mistaken. It is free only during parliamentary elections: once the members of Parliament have been elected it lapses back into slavery, and becomes as nothing."[2] The recall attempts to solve this problem. It allows a certain minimum number of voters who are dissatisfied with their representative to ask for a special election in which the representative can be removed. This device can only work in plurality and majority electoral systems, because it requires that each representative's constituents can be clearly identified. Hence it is incompatible with proportional or semiproportional representation.

4. Direct primary elections circumvent the political parties as intermediaries in the electoral process. They take the selection of candidates out of the hands of the party organizations and their formal membership and give it to the entire electorate. The crucial characteristic of direct primaries is that they "permit any one voter who *declares himself* to be a member of a party to vote

2. Jean Jacques Rousseau, *The Social Contract*, trans. Willmoore Kendall (Chicago: Henry Regnery, 1954), p. 108.

in that party's primary. He assumes no obligation to the party to acquire this power, and the party has no power to exclude him from participation in selecting its candidates."[3] Direct primaries make party labels more important than party organizations.

Most of these four instruments of direct democracy are extremely rare, and most democracies have remained solidly representative. In our twenty-two democratic regimes, the recall is not used anywhere at the national level. Primaries occur exclusively in the United States. Popularly elected chief executives are found only in the United States, France, and Finland. The voters have the right of initiative at the national level only in Switzerland and Italy; the initiative is also important in California and some other states, but not at the federal level in the United States. The referendum, however, has been used in a majority of the democracies. It will be the subject of the remainder of this chapter.

REFERENDUMS

Table 12.1 shows the number of referendums—that is, the number of issues on which the voters have been able to vote in national referendums—in twenty-two democracies from 1945 to 1980. The most striking aspect of the table is the extreme unevenness of the incidence of referendums. Switzerland accounts for more than two-thirds of the total, whereas not a single referendum was held in nine of the countries. But there is also a general pattern that emerges from the table: the relative rarity of the referendum in all countries except Switzerland. Even in Australia and New Zealand, the second and third most frequent users of the referendum, it has occurred only once every other year on the average in the 1945–80 period.

3. Austin Ranney, "Candidate Selection," in David Butler, Howard R. Penniman, and Austin Ranney, eds., *Democracy at the Polls: A Comparative Study of Competitive National Elections* (Washington, D.C.: American Enterprise Institute, 1981), p. 86.

TABLE 12.1. National Referendums and Provisions for Mandatory and Optional Constitutional Referendums in 22 Democracies, 1945–1980

	Number of referendum issues			Constitutional referendum
	Total	1945–62	1963–80	
Switzerland	169	67	102	Mandatory
Australia	18	5	13	Mandatory
New Zealand	17	9	8	
Denmark	11	3	8	Mandatory
Ireland	8	1	7	Mandatory
France V	6	4	2	Optional
France IV	4	4	—	Optional
Italy	4	1	3	Optional
Sweden	3	1	2	
Austria	1	0	1	Optional
Belgium	1	1	0	
Norway	1	0	1	
United Kingdom	1	0	1	
Canada	0	0	0	
Finland	0	0	0	
Germany	0	0	0	
Iceland	0	0	0	
Israel	0	0	0	
Japan	0	0	0	Mandatory
Luxembourg	0	0	0	
Netherlands	0	0	0	
United States	0	0	0	

Source: Adapted from David Butler and Austin Ranney, eds., *Referendums: A Comparative Study of Practice and Theory* (Washington, D.C.: American Enterprise Institute, 1978), pp. 57–64, 127–28, 227–37; and *Keesing's Contemporary Archives* (London: Keesing's Publications).

On the other hand, its use is becoming somewhat more frequent. David Butler and Austin Ranney discern a "slow but unmistakeable growth in the number of referendums" since about 1900, which "has accelerated a bit since 1960."[4] The figures for the period from 1945 to 1980 in table 12.1 confirm the existence

4. David Butler and Austin Ranney, "Summing Up," in David Butler and Austin Ranney, eds., *Referendums: A Comparative Study of Practice and Theory* (Washington, D.C.: American Enterprise Institute, 1978), p. 221.

of such a trend. In all countries except Switzerland, there were 29 referendums during the first half of this period and 46 in the second half. And in Switzerland, too, the use of the referendum increased from 67 to 102 from the first to the second half of the period under consideration. It should also be pointed out, however, that of the nine countries without any referendums between 1945 and 1980, five—Canada, Finland, Germany, Iceland, and Luxembourg—did have one or more before 1945. Referendums are clearly not addictive.

In order to determine the extent to which referendums really serve the function of increasing direct popular influence, they can be classified according to two criteria proposed by Gordon Smith: controlled vs. uncontrolled, and pro-hegemonic vs. anti-hegemonic referendums. A referendum is controlled if the government can decide whether or not to hold it, when it will take place, and how the question will be asked. If a referendum is originated by a popular initiative, it is by definition uncontrolled. In Smith's words, "it can be assumed that strong control will only be associated with referenda that have foreseeable results in favour of the governing authority. The reverse applies for an 'uncontrolled' referendum: the whole point of a popular initiative is to bring about changes which for one reason or another are resisted by the government." The second criterion concerns not the right of initiation and the intended result, but the actual result: a referendum is pro-hegemonic or anti-hegemonic depending on whether its consequences are "supportive or detrimental to a regime."[5]

Most referendums are both controlled and pro-hegemonic. One reason is that the initiative is available in only very few countries. And when governments control the referendum, they will tend to use it only when they expect to win. Political circumstances other than the emergence of initiatives may also constrain governments, of course. An example is the 1972 Nor-

5. Gordon Smith, "The Functional Properties of the Referendum," *European Journal of Political Research* 4, no. 1 (March 1976): 6.

wegian referendum on European Community membership. Parliament was overwhelmingly favorable and could have acted without popular approval, but there was a strong feeling that on an issue of this nature and importance a parliamentary vote alone would have been illegitimate. The voters rejected Norway's entry into the European Community against the advice of the political establishment. The Norwegian referendum is therefore an example of an only partially controlled and clearly anti-hegemonic referendum. Another set of not fully controlled referendums are those that are mandatory for constitutional amendments: if a government strongly desires such an amendment, it can control its wording and the timing of the referendum but not whether or not to let the referendum take place.

Not all controlled referendums turn out to be pro-hegemonic, since governments sometimes miscalculate popular support. The prime example is the entirely controlled referendum on the reform of the Senate and local government in France in 1969. President Charles de Gaulle did not have to call it, and he did not have to link his political fate with it. When it lost, he resigned at once. On the whole, however, referendums tend to win rather than lose. They are political weapons in the hands of governments rather than weapons against governments.

THE PATTERN OF USAGE OF REFERENDUMS

How can we account for the incidence of referendums in democracies? As table 12.1 shows, thirteen of our twenty-two countries made little or no use of the referendum in the 1945–80 period (that is, they held no or only one referendum), while the other nine were occasional to very frequent users. Five possible explanations must be considered—and rejected.

1. On the basis of our theoretical discussion of majoritarian and consensus democracy, we would not expect the incidence of referendums to be related to the characteristics of either model. The next chapter will show that there is indeed no such link.

2. Ivor Crewe regards referendums as one element of the "range of participation" available to the voters. How many opportunities the voters have to participate at the national level also depends on how frequently first-chamber elections are held and whether or not other national officeholders, such as members of the second chamber and presidents, are popularly elected.[6] Crewe's analysis suggests two plausible hypotheses. Referendums may be either positively or negatively related to the range of participation: they may be part of a syndrome of frequent and varied voting opportunities, or they may serve as a compensation for a relative dearth of other chances to participate. Both hypotheses have to be rejected. The thirteen countries with little or no use of the referendum and the nine that use it occasionally to frequently have virtually identical average election frequencies as far as their first chambers are concerned, nor do they differ with regard to other national voting opportunities.

3. Butler and Ranney explain the fact that referendums are widely used only in Switzerland and several states in the United States in terms of their "long-standing prereferendum experience with direct government by face-to-face assemblies of citizens." When population growth made such assemblies impractical, the referendum and initiative "came into being as useful ways of adapting the principles of direct democracy to the limitations and necessities of large populations."[7] This is a valid but very limited explanation: it explains why Switzerland appears at the top of the list in table 12.1 but not the variation among the other twenty-one democracies.

4. Another relevant factor identified by Butler and Ranney is whether or not the referendum is accompanied by the initiative. The availability of the initiative "helps to explain" why a few countries and states "have had so many more referendums

<hr>

6. Ivor Crewe, "Electoral Participation," in Butler et al., Democracy at the Polls, pp. 225–32.

7. David Butler and Austin Ranney, "Practice," in Butler et al., Referendums, p. 6.

than all other democratic polities."[8] The initiative renders the referendum uncontrolled and hence more frequent. Of the twenty-two democracies in table 12.1 only two—Switzerland and Italy—have the initiative. They are indeed both in the occasional-to-frequent category, but Butler and Ranney's explanation does not account for the variation among the remaining twenty countries.

5. Finally, Butler and Ranney point out that the subject matter of referendums has been "overwhelmingly constitutional."[9] This suggests that we should expect referendums especially in those countries in which constitutional amendments require approval by referendum, and to a certain extent also in countries where a referendum is one of the options for constitutional change. These provisions are indicated in table 12.1. Here a clear pattern emerges: seven of the nine occasional-to-frequent users of the referendum, but only two of the thirteen others, have a mandatory or optional constitutional referendum.

Upon further reflection, this last explanation cannot be considered satisfactory either. It immediately raises the question: why do the constitutions of some but not all democracies require or permit the referendum for constitutional change? Constitutions express certain philosophies of government. To explain political patterns in terms of constitutional prescriptions is largely tautological. Although it is difficult for social scientists to admit defeat in the search for general propositions and theories, we are forced to agree with Butler and Ranney that referendums "fail to fit any clear universal pattern."[10]

8. Butler and Ranney, "Summing Up," p. 222.
9. Butler and Ranney, "Practice," p. 10.
10. Ibid., p. 18.

Rational, Prescriptive, and Empirical Models of Democracy

13

This book has systematically contrasted the two basic models of democracy. The term *model* can be, and has been, used in three different senses: rational, prescriptive, and empirical. This final chapter will look more closely at the question of precisely what kinds of models the majoritarian and consensus models may be said to be. The main emphasis will be on the extent to which they are empirical ones.

RATIONAL MODELS

In the first place, the majoritarian and consensus models of democracy are rational and logically coherent. Chapters 1 and 2 introduced the two models by example and by contrast. The majoritarian model was described with the help of the British and New Zealand examples. The consensus model was described as the opposite of the majoritarian, and as exemplified by the Swiss and Belgian democratic regimes. It is also possible, however, to derive all of the characteristics of the majoritarian model logically from the principle of concentrating as much political power as possible in the hands of the majority. Conversely, all of the characteristics of the consensus model logically follow from the premise that political power should be dispersed and shared in a variety of ways.

With regard to the arrangement of executive power, for instance, if one wants to maximize the concentration of power, the logical method is to give all of it to a one-party cabinet supported by a strong and cohesive majority in parliament. On the other hand, the maximum degree of the sharing of power can be achieved by a grand coalition of all the parties, none of which holds a majority of the parliamentary seats. The electoral system that maximizes the concentration of power in the hands of the majority is the plurality method. The greatest dispersal of power can be attained by proportional representation without electoral threshold in a single national district.

The two rational models do not always coincide with the logical extremes on each dimension. Limits are imposed both by what is practical and by what is appropriate to the conditions of particular countries. A good example of practical limits is the organization of the legislature. The logical method to maximize the concentration of power is unicameralism. The logical extreme on the other end of this dimension would be a legislature consisting of very many chambers—in principle, approaching infinity—all with equal legislative powers and all differently constituted. Such an arrangement is obviously unworkable, and the practical limit in modern democracies is a strong bicameralism rather than multicameralism. Similarly, with regard to federalism and decentralization, the logical extreme on the consensual side would be a federal system in which the component units have all the power and the central government none; but this spells partition rather than strong federalism. The logical extreme of an optimally rigid constitution with a veto for every conceivable small minority would be a completely unamendable one—again a most impractical setup.

The conditions of a particular society may entail additional limits. For example, the logical extremes on the dimension of the party system are a strict two-party system and a multiparty system with as many parties as there are seats in the legislature. The latter extreme is not only impractical but also fails the test of appropriateness. The pure consensus model requires multipartism, with a sufficient number of parties to represent all of the natural social cleavages and divisions of opinion instead of a boundless and senseless proliferation of parties.

The above examples all concern the consensual side of the dimensions differentiating the two models. On the majoritarian side, the logical extremes are indeed usually also practical possibilities: a minimal winning one-party cabinet, a predominant executive, unicameralism, a pure two-party system with one issue dimension dividing the two parties, unitary and completely centralized government, and an unwritten constitution. The only exception is the dimension of the electoral system. There the logical extreme is not the single-member-district plurality method but plurality applied at large in a single national district. If there were two dominant and cohesive parties, and if the voters voted straight tickets, the party winning a plurality of the votes would not just win a disproportional number of the seats but all of the seats in the legislature. Such at-large plurality elections may not be completely impractical, but they favor the majority to a degree that few majoritarians would be willing to defend.

PRESCRIPTIVE MODELS

The majoritarian and consensus models are also prescriptive. They entail a set of basic choices that have to be made by democratic constitutional engineers in countries that attempt to introduce or strengthen a democratic regime. Wherever problems of deep differences and tensions between groups in society form a challenge to stable and effective democracy, consensual solutions are to be recommended. It is significant that the major deviations from the majoritarian model in Great Britain and New Zealand have to do with the fact that neither is a completely homogeneous society; in particular, the role of the Scottish National party, the plans for a degree of autonomy for Scotland, British policy in Northern Ireland, and the special protection of the Maori minority in New Zealand are more consensual than majoritarian.

One additional difference between the two prescriptive models should be kept in mind. The majoritarian model approximates a constitutional blueprint, whereas the consensus model merely supplies the general principles on which constitutional provisions can be based but which entail a number of further choices that have to be made. With regard to the electoral system, for example, the majoritarian model prescribes single-member-district plurality elections; once the size of the legislature has been determined, this prescription can be implemented at once. However, the consensual prescription of proportional representation requires additional and very important decisions on which of the many formulas of proportional representation should be adopted, whether a system of supplementary seats should be used, and how large the electoral districts should be. Similarly, with regard to constitutional change, the majoritarian model simply prescribes an unwritten constitution and parliamentary sovereignty, which means pure majority rule and no minority veto at all. The consensual prescription of a rigid constitution with a veto power for minorities can only be implemented after a decision has been reached on whether the veto should take the form of an extraordinary majority in parliament and/or of regional governments, the size of the special majority, and so on. As far as judicial review is concerned, the majoritarian decision not to adopt it is a simple one, whereas the consensual desire to institute it entails the choice between its centralized and decentralized forms.

This characteristic of consensus democracy appears to make it a more difficult model to apply than the simpler majoritarian model. On the other hand, it contains the great advantage that the consensual model can be adapted to suit the special needs of particular countries. It can also give constitutional engineers the option of building onto existing legitimate traditions. Hence the simplicity of the majoritarian model is counterbalanced by the flexibility of the consensual one.

Societal conditions will frequently be serious constraints on constitutional engineers and prevent them from exercising a completely free choice between the alternative models. For instance, in a society with several distinct and geographically concentrated ethnic or cultural minorities, a two-party system may not only be undesirable but also completely impossible; the single-member-district plurality method of election is certainly not a sufficient means to bring it about. On the other hand, if these minorities should be geographically interspersed, the consensual ideal of incongruent federalism cannot be instituted.

EMPIRICAL MODELS

Since the majoritarian and consensus models of democracy are rational and logically coherent models, we can also expect them to be empirical ones. That is, since the eight majoritarian characteristics are derived from the same principle and hence are logically connected, we may also expect them to occur together in the real world; the same applies to the eight consensual elements. But the ninth characteristic, exclusively representative democracy, should not be related to the other eight. Is this actually the case in our twenty-two democracies? Chapters 1 and 2 argued that, with a few exceptions and qualifications, the eight characteristics did cluster very neatly in the four illustrative examples of the United Kingdom, New Zealand, Switzerland, and Belgium. Subsequent chapters have revealed the clustering of several elements in all or most of the twenty-two countries. The final two sections of this chapter will try to discover the overall empirical patterns among all twenty-two countries; we shall look both for clusters of related characteristics and for clusters of similar democratic regimes.

Factor analysis is the most suitable method for detecting whether there are one or more common underlying dimensions among several variables. It requires that the data be in interval form. This is already the case for most of our nine characteristics treated in chapters 4 through 12, but a few adjustments and additional operational definitions are needed:

1. Minimal winning cabinets. We shall use the adjusted percentages of the time during which minimal winning cabinets were in power in twenty-one democracies (see table 4.2). The United States was not included in the table, as it does not have a cabinet dependent on parliamentary confidence. For the factor analysis, it will be given a score of 100, indicating the absence of any coalition cabinets. Occasionally, members of the other party have been appointed by presidents, but never in sufficient numbers for the equal or proportional participation of both parties typical of true coalition cabinets. Richard F. Fenno, Jr., states: "Typically, the entire Cabinet is of the same political party as the President. . . . The few exceptions serve only to prove the rule. Many deviations from this norm are more apparent than real, involving men whose ideas and sympathies obviously do not coincide with their partisan labels."[1]

2. Executive dominance. This characteristic will be measured in terms of the average cabinet durability in twenty countries listed in table 5.3, but four additions and adjustments have to be made for the four democracies that are not purely parliamentary regimes. A score of 30, indicating a balanced executive–legislative relationship, will be assigned to Finland, Switzerland, and the United States, and a score of 60, showing a high degree of executive dominance, to the French Fifth Republic.

3. Unicameralism. The final classification of chapter 6 was a qualitative one, but it can easily be transformed into a quanti-

1. Richard F. Fenno, Jr., *The President's Cabinet: An Analysis in the Period from Wilson to Eisenhower* (Cambridge, Mass.: Harvard University Press, 1959), p. 68.

tative index. The following scores will be used: 4 for unicameralism, 3 for congruent and extremely asymmetrical bicameralism, 2 for incongruent and extremely asymmetrical bicameralism, 1 for congruent and symmetrical or moderately asymetrical bicameralism, and 0 for strong bicameralism. Sweden, unicameral since 1970 but bicameral before that, will receive a score of 3.

4. Effective number of parties. Table 7.3 provides all of the necessary data.[2]

5. Number of issue dimensions. The data will be taken from the last column of table 8.1.

6. Electoral disproportionality. The data are the indices of disproportionality shown in table 9.1.

7. Centralization. This characteristic will be measured in terms of the central governments' shares of tax receipts, shown in table 10.2. No comparable information is available for the Fourth French Republic, but most observers agree that in this respect no major changes have accompanied the shift from the Fourth to the Fifth Republic. Hence it will be assigned the same value of 88 percent.

8. Constitutional flexibility. A score of 3 will be assigned to an unwritten constitution. From this maximum, 1 point will be subtracted for the existence of a written constitution, for a rigid constitution with minority veto, and for active judicial review; 0.5 point (instead of a full point) will be subtracted for the sole requirement of a referendum to amend the constitution, for relatively infrequent judicial review, as well as for the recent and

2. For the number-of-parties and number-of-issue-dimensions variables, the signs of all values have to be reversed in order to give the highest value to the majoritarian characteristic—in accordance with the scoring of all of the other variables.

TABLE 13.1. Varimax Rotated Factor Matrix of the Nine
Variables Distinguishing Majoritarian from
Consensus Democracy

Variable	Factor I	Factor II
Minimal winning cabinets	.85	.04
Executive dominance	.72	−.06
Effective number of parties	.99	−.10
Number of issue dimensions	.75	.02
Electoral disproportionality	.42	−.03
Unicameralism	.01	.65
Centralization	−.14	.51
Constitutional flexibility	−.12	.76
Referendums	−.01	−.02

not fully developed kind of judicial review in the French Fifth
Republic. This means that countries with a written and rigid
constitution guarded by full judicial review will be assigned the
lowest score of 0.

9. Referendums. This characteristic will be scored as if the
absence of referendums were a feature of the Westminster model.
The countries with no referendums from 1945 to 1980 will therefore be given the maximum score of 4 and Switzerland the lowest
score of 0. In between, a score of 1 will be given to frequent
referendums (those with 6 to 18 referendums in table 12.1), 2 to
occasional (three or four) referendums, and 3 to countries with
only one referendum experience. Because all four referendums
in the French Fourth Republic had to do with the adoption of its
constitution, it will also be given the score of 3.

The results of the factor analysis are presented in table 13.1.
Contrary to the hypothesis of a single cluster of majoritarian vs.
consensual characteristics, suggested by the two models as rational models, we find two clearly different and unrelated empirical clusters. The previous chapters, of course, had already
intimated such a pattern. The first factor virtually coincides with

the effective number of parties: the factor loading, which may be interpreted as the correlation coefficient between the number-of-parties variable and the first factor, is a near perfect .99. Minimal winning cabinets, executive dominance, and the number of issue dimensions are also closely related to it. The degree of electoral disproportionality is a relatively weaker part of the cluster. The second factor groups together the characteristics of unicameralism, centralization, and constitutional flexibility. All three were shown in previous chapters to be closely related to federalism. The referendum variable behaves as hypothesized: it is totally unrelated to either factor.

CLUSTERS OF COUNTRIES

How do our twenty-two democratic regimes cluster on the two underlying dimensions of the majoritarian-consensual contrast? A first attempt at an overall classification is made in table 13.2. It presents the standardized factor scores for each country on the two dimensions. These scores can be interpreted as averages of the values of the original variables, weighted proportionally according to their involvement in the factor.[3] The countries are grouped into four categories based on the signs of the factor scores. The group of six purely majoritarian regimes have positive scores on both dimensions; the five purely consensual regimes score negatively on the two dimensions. In addition, there are six countries that are positive on the first but negative on the second dimension. Because of the close connection between the second dimension and federalism, this category is labeled "majoritarian-federal"; five of the six regimes are indeed federal, but the group also includes unitary, but decentralized, Japan. Similarly, the fourth group of five countries is labeled "consensual-unitary" because they score negatively on the first but positively on the second, federal, dimension.

3. See R. J. Rummel, "Understanding Factor Analysis," *Journal of Conflict Resolution* 11, no. 4 (December 1967): 469–70.

TABLE 13.2. Standardized Factor Scores for 22 Democratic
Regimes

	Factor I	Factor II
Majoritarian		
New Zealand	1.42	2.11
United Kingdom	1.16	1.56
Ireland	.61	.20
Luxembourg	.08	.75
Sweden	.48	.31
Norway	.42	.09
Majoritarian-federal		
United States	1.11	−1.38
Canada	.81	−1.01
Germany	.68	−1.55
Austria	1.50	−.65
Australia	.67	−.97
Japan	.12	−.98
Consensual-unitary		
Israel	−1.07	1.75
Denmark	−.78	.56
Finland	−1.49	.33
France IV	−1.52	.29
Iceland	−.06	1.05
Consensual		
Switzerland	−1.65	−1.19
Belgium	−.55	−.48
Netherlands	−1.69	−.06
Italy	−.10	−.66
France V	−.18	−.09

The factor scores in table 13.2 are standardized with a mean
of 0 and a standard deviation of 1. Scores close to 0 indicate an
intermediate position on the factor, and the scores greater than 1
or less than −1, approximately a third of the total, show a very
strong position. There are only five countries with very strong
scores on both dimensions; they are the prototypes of the different categories. Prototypical of the majoritarian group are New
Zealand and the United Kingdom, in line with the argument of

chapter 1. The extremely high scores of New Zealand and the relatively less impressive British scores also confirm the contention of chapter 1 that New Zealand is a more nearly perfect example of the Westminster model than the country of the Westminster model's origin.

The consensual prototype is Switzerland, in accordance with the argument of chapter 2. However, the other representative example of the consensual model used in chapter 2, Belgium, cannot be considered a prototype on the basis of its factor scores. This is to some extent a result of our operational definitions; as pointed out earlier, for instance, our definition of oversized coalitions in terms of political parties does not take into account that Belgian cabinets are permanent ethnic grand coalitions, and our measure of centralization does not reflect Belgium's sociological federalism (see chapters 4 and 10). Its merely moderate score on the second dimension also indicates that it is a semifederal rather than a fully federal regime. As it continues the process of federalization, this score is likely to become more strongly negative. Similarly, Belgium's score on the first dimension will become stronger if the strong multipartism and the frequent oversized coalition cabinets of the 1970s turn into lasting features of the political system. There are no other countries in the consensual category that approach prototypical status. The Netherlands has a very high score on the first factor but close to a zero score on the federal dimension. Apart from Switzerland, Belgium is the only country with at least moderately strong negative scores on both dimensions.

Chapter 2 used the United States as the example of an intermediate and frequently deviant political system, exhibiting some majoritarian and some consensual characteristics. Table 13.2 shows it to be the prototype of the new majoritarian-federal category, not foreseen by chapter 2. Its very strong negative score on the second dimension reflects a strong position on all three variables that form the basis of this dimension: decentralized federalism, strong bicameralism, and a rigid constitution combined with active judicial review. On the five variables of the first dimension, the United States is strongly majoritarian with one exception: it has a balanced system of executive–legislative relations rather than the majoritarian ideal of executive dominance. Three other countries in the majoritarian-federal category—Canada, Germany, and Austria—also have scores higher than 1 or lower than −1 on one of the dimensions, but not on both.

The prototypical example of the new consensual-unitary category is Israel. As the preceding chapters have shown, it is without exception strongly consensual on all five variables of the first dimension, but even more clearly majoritarian or unitary on the second dimension, as a result of its highly centralized government, unicameral legislature, and unwritten constitution. Three other countries have strong scores on one of the dimensions but much weaker scores on the other: Finland, the French Fourth Republic, and Iceland. Denmark is listed as the second case in the consensual-unitary group because it has moderately high scores on both factors.

The fourfold classification of table 13.2 performs the useful function of identifying the prototypes of each class, but it is not a satisfactory method for categorizing the countries that have much weaker scores on one or both dimensions. For instance, the French Fifth Republic is listed in the consensual category on the basis of its two negative scores, but these scores are both so weak that its assignment to one of the four groups is almost purely accidental. In order to recognize the intermediate cases with low scores on one or both dimensions, we need a ninefold classification. Such a classification is presented in table 13.3. The cut-off point for the intermediate scores were set at −.50 and .50, half of a standard deviation around the mean. These values were chosen somewhat but not completely arbitrarily: they divide the twenty-two democratic regimes into three groups of roughly equal size on each dimension.

Almost half, ten out of twenty-two, of the countries clearly belong to one of the four principal types of democracy. Three

TABLE 13.3. Nine Clusters of Democratic Regimes

		Dimension II		
		Majoritarian	*Intermediate*	*Consensual*
Dimension I	*Majoritarian*	New Zealand United Kingdom	Ireland	Australia *Austria* Canada Germany *United States*
	Intermediate	Iceland *Luxembourg*	*France V* Norway Sweden	Italy Japan
	Consensual	Denmark *Israel*	*Belgium* *Finland* *France IV* *Netherlands*	*Switzerland*

Note: (1) The plural and semiplural societies are italicized. (2) The intermediate category encompasses countries with factor scores between − .50 and .50.

countries are in the middle cell, with intermediate scores on both factors: the Fifth French Republic is joined by Norway and Sweden. Nine countries are in classes characterized by one intermediate classification. Belgium is in one of these rather than in the same class as Switzerland, since its score of − .48 on the federal dimension is slightly above the − .50 dividing line. Switzerland is the sole occupant of the purely consensual category. The other three classes at the corners of the matrix are more densely populated. They contain all of the prototypical cases, of course, but the consensual-unitary group includes Denmark in addition to Israel, and the majoritarian-federal group includes four federal regimes in addition to the United States.

Clearly, the majoritarian-federal category is a very important one empirically, although it is a mixture of two logically opposite models of democracy. The fact that several countries have successfully combined majoritarian and consensual-federal features demonstrates that the two opposite sets of characteristics are not incompatible. The only serious conflict may be the one between minimal winning cabinets in a parliamentary system and strong bicameralism in which the two chambers have differently constituted majorities. In chapter 6, this problem was dismissed as reflecting a majoritarian bias, but it may indeed lead to potentially very serious crises if these two majoritarian and consensual features are combined in a single regime, as in Australia and Germany. The two obvious solutions represent a retreat from the pure type on one of the dimensions. The United States exemplifies one solution: its majoritarianism on the first dimension is tempered by its separation of powers and resultant executive–legislative equilibrium. Austria and Canada are examples of the other solution: their consensual character on the federal dimension is moderated by a weaker bicameralism, in which the second chamber is inferior to the first chamber.

How can we account for the clustering of the twenty-two regimes that we find in table 13.3? The table suggests three causal explanations, all of which have already been mentioned in earlier chapters: the degree of pluralism, population size, and cultural influence. First, there is a clear, although not perfect, relationship between the degree to which the countries are plural societies and their type of regime. The plural and semiplural societies are italicized in table 13.3. As we move from the upper left-hand cell to the lower right-hand cell, we encounter plural and semiplural societies with increasing frequency. Nonplural Japan and plural Luxembourg are the most obvious deviant cases.

Second, our earlier analysis in chapter 6 found a strong link between the size of a country's population and the incidence of bicameralism or unicameralism: small population size and unicameralism (or insignificant bicameralism) tended to go together. Table 13.3 shows that population size is more generally linked to the entire second dimension of the majoritarian-consensual contrast, of which the variable of unicameralism vs. bicameralism is one of the components. If we divide our twenty-one countries into eleven small and ten large countries, as in chapter 6, we find that the left-hand column contains only small countries with one exception (the United Kingdom), that the right-hand column contains only large countries with two exceptions (Austria and Switzerland), and that the middle column contains large and small countries in equal proportions. The United Kingdom is a strikingly deviant case, but Austria and Switzerland are among the three largest, together with Sweden, of the small countries.

The third explanation applies to the classification of the twenty-two regimes according to the first dimension. Our earlier discussion, especially at the end of chapter 4, called attention to the strong influence of the Westminster model in countries having a British cultural heritage. Table 13.3 shows an almost perfect dichotomy between Anglo-American countries, in the top row of the table, and all other countries, in the middle and bottom rows. The only exceptions are Austria and Germany, but especially in the latter case, we should remember the strong influence on postwar German politics of the United States and Britain as occupying powers. Two other regional-cultural groupings, the Nordic and Benelux countries, are clustered in the four lower left-hand cells of the matrix.

Thus, the classification of table 13.3 represents a grand summary of the findings of this book, but it is also necessarily a very rough summary. For one thing, it summarizes the political characteristics of democratic regimes over the long time span from 1945 to 1980—more than a third of a century—and it may mask temporal trends and fluctuations. France is the one exception because we have treated the Fourth and Fifth Republics as separate cases, and the two Republics are located in different but adjacent categories of table 13.3. It should be remembered, however, that the transition to the Fifth Republic entailed a deliberate change of regime by constitutional engineers who detested the Fourth Republic. Belgium has undergone a similar deliberate, but more gradual, constitutional transformation since about 1970. For most of the countries, however, the classification is based on structural characteristics that are quite stable, even though obviously not immobile, over time. Hence they can be said to occupy firm positions on the two-dimensional pattern of majoritarian and consensus democracy.

Index